SNAKES

Look for these and other books in the
Lucent Endangered Animals and Habitats Series:

The Amazon Rain Forest
The Bald Eagle
The Bear
Birds of Prey
Coral Reefs
The Cougar
The Elephant
The Giant Panda
The Gorilla
The Jaguar
The Manatee
The Oceans
The Orangutan
The Rhinoceros
Seals and Sea Lions
The Shark
Snakes
The Tiger
Turtles and Tortoises
The Whale
The Wolf

Other related titles in the Lucent Overview Series:

Acid Rain
Endangered Species
Energy Alternatives
Garbage
The Greenhouse Effect
Hazardous Waste
Ocean Pollution
Oil Spills
Ozone
Pesticides
Population
Rainforests
Recycling
Saving the American Wilderness
Vanishing Wetlands
Zoos

SNAKES

BY KELLY L. BARTH

Endangered
Animals &
Habitats

LUCENT BOOKS, INC.
SAN DIEGO, CALIFORNIA

Library of Congress Cataloging-in-Publication Data

Barth, Kelly L.
  Snakes / by Kelly L. Barth.
    p. cm. — (Endangered animals & habitats)
  Includes bibliographical references and index.
  ISBN 1-56006-696-2 (hardcover : alk. paper)
  1. Snakes—Juvenile literature. 2. Endangered species—Juvenile
literature. [1. Snakes. 2. Endangered species.] I. Title. II. Series.
  QL666.O6 B3285 2001
  597.96—dc21

                                        00-009839

Contents

Introduction

MORE THAN MOST other creatures, snakes have captured the imaginations of human beings. However, many city-dwelling people have never even seen one of these mysterious and elusive creatures. Despite whether people see snakes in the wild, they are most certainly aware of their existence. And whether they evoke fear, awe, or admiration, snakes play a vital role in the natural world.

Snakes in myth and symbol

The presence of snakes in the mythology of most of the world's cultures illustrates the fascination snakes have held for people over the millennia. One of the more familiar myths featuring the snake is the biblical story of Satan taking the form of a snake and tempting Eve to eat the forbidden fruit from the tree of knowledge. In many other myths as well, snakes represent the evil forces that humans must contend with on Earth. However, in the mythology of other cultures, snakes represent positive qualities or events, including fertility, birth, and the creation of the earth or of a particular culture.

Whether people believed they were good or evil, snakes have universally symbolized great power to humans. For example, though the colonists who settled North America feared the bite of the rattlesnake, perhaps because of that fear they later included the rattler on the Revolutionary War flag with the phrase "Don't Tread on Me" to indicate that they, like the snake, would kill to protect their home.

For many people, snakes evoke nothing but fear, however unfounded. Certainly, some snakes can bite and injure or kill people, but such occurrences are quite rare. For instance, more people in the United States are killed each year by lightning or bee stings than by snake bites.

Friends of humans

Researchers now know that although some species are potentially deadly to humans and merit respect, snakes, as a group, help humans in many ways. For example, snakes control populations of rodents that, if allowed to reproduce freely, would devastate some food crops. Snakes also help prevent the spread of devastating human diseases. As herpetologists Carl H. Ernst and George R. Zug say, "If rodent control by nonvenomous and venomous snakes is reduced, human exposure to rats and hence to the plague bacillus rises. Recently a new threat, the hantavirus, has appeared in the Southwest and in Florida. That rodents are the prime vector for this virus represents another reason to protect snakes for purposes of rodent control."[1] Also, by controlling some insects, snakes reduce the need for applying

Snakes have continually been portrayed as a source of power and strength despite human fear of them. The rattlesnake, for example, was chosen as an emblem for the American revolutionary war flag in 1775.

A Peruvian red-tailed boa constrictor preys on a rat. Snakes are helpful in controlling rodent populations.

chemical pesticides that can harm both people and other creatures in the environment.

The decline of snakes

Despite the growing recognition of their positive role, populations of many snake species are on the decline. The primary reason for such a drop in numbers is human alteration and contamination of snake habitats. Wetlands and waterways have been drained and dammed, destroying crucial habitats for many snake species in the process. Other snakes have lost their homes as woodlands are logged and as what was formerly prairie and grassland has been converted to agriculture. Pesticides applied to agricultural fields have also contributed to the contamination of surrounding snake habitats. Likewise, as a growing human population develops land for housing and roads, it encroaches upon snake habitats. As snakes come into ever closer contact with humans, they are inadvertently and intentionally killed.

Hope for the future

Though the future is cloudy for many snake species, humans have begun to address the problems that they cause snakes. They have looked at ways to preserve snake habitats and to use land in ways that are less destructive to the species at risk. Researchers are looking for ways to adapt industry, agriculture, and forestry to the needs of threatened snakes as well.

Legislation also protects endangered snakes. For instance, the U.S. Endangered Species Act, which was passed in 1973, protects animals, including snakes, in danger of becoming extinct. Within the Endangered Species Act, endangered animals are distinguished from threatened ones. To be listed as endangered, a species must be in danger of extinction throughout most of its natural range. An animal is listed as threatened if, because of low population and problems with reproduction, it stands a good chance of becoming endangered in the near future.

For endangered and threatened species, public education campaigns can mean the difference between extinction and survival. When people become more familiar with snakes, they become less fearful of them and sometimes even go so far as to try to protect them and their habitats. Programs to build such awareness have been and will continue to be needed in areas where endangered snakes live.

Even scientists have much to learn about snakes. In fact, until they can fine-tune methods of surveying the health, habits, and population size of these elusive creatures, scientists can do little to help many endangered snakes. This field of research remains open for researchers with the time, energy, and creativity for the task.

1

What Is a Snake?

THE SNAKE'S ANCESTRY can be traced back to lizards that lived about 130 million years ago. Scientists believe that these reptiles began to evolve into limbless creatures resembling snakes in order to tunnel underground in search of food. This adaptation contributed to their survival in other ways as well. For example, they could easily retreat underground to escape from predators. By the Pleistocene era, about 1.8 million years ago, these burrowing creatures had evolved into the variety of snake species living today.

The success of the snake's adaptation is evidenced by the fact that snakes live everywhere, except in high mountain areas and in Antarctica, where it is too cold for them to survive. Also, if given adequate protection, they can flourish in nearly every type of environment on Earth, including grasslands, swamps, forests, and even developed areas such as suburbs.

Orders and families

Although snakes are a widely distributed and diverse group, all snakes belong to the class scientists call Reptilia (reptiles). Along with lizards, snakes belong to the order Squamata, which arises from the Latin word *squama,* meaning "scales." Snakes have a suborder of their own called Serpentes (serpents).

Most scientists break the suborder Serpentes down into ten smaller groupings, called families. Whereas some of these families have numerous species of snakes, others have only one. Within these ten families there are nearly twenty-six hundred snake species living around the world. The best known families are the Boidae, Colubridae, Elapidae, and Viperidae.

Boidae

Boas and pythons belong to the family Boidae, which includes some of the largest snakes in the world. For example, the anaconda, a boa, grows to be nearly twenty feet long and can weigh up to three hundred pounds. Another good example of a boidae is the reticulated python, which, measuring up to thirty-two feet long, is the largest snake in the world. Though the reticulated python eats small mammals, it is capable of eating pigs, deer, and even people. Boas live in Central, South, and North America; pythons live in Africa, Southeast Asia, and Australia.

Boas, like this Jamaican boa, live in Central, South, and North America.

Boas, which are confined to the New World, and pythons, which are confined to the Old World, are generally grouped together because they kill their prey by constricting it. First, they seize prey with their mouths, then coil around their victim and squeeze, causing their prey's lungs to collapse and heart to constrict.

Colubridae

Three-fourths of the world's snakes belong to the family Colubridae. Colubrids live in a variety of places, including trees, grasses, and water, and they hunt a variety of small prey, such as frogs, mice, rats, rabbits, and insects. Some examples of colubrids are garter, rat, corn, fox, grass, smooth, racer, water, king, hognose, and gopher snakes.

One general similarity snakes in this family share is that most are nonpoisonous. In the rare cases that a colubrid does have venom, its bite is usually not life-threatening. The few poisonous colubrids are all rear-fanged snakes and so must get a large initial bite on their prey if they are to inject venom. Their venom does not kill the prey but only paralyzes it. Some examples of poisonous colubrids are vine snakes, flying snakes, the boomslang, and African birdsnake.

Elapidae

Snakes belonging to the family Elapidae are exclusively poisonous and live mainly in Africa, India, Asia, and Australia. The most common members of the Elapidae family are cobras and mambas. Some examples of elapids are the king cobra, the world's largest poisonous snake; the Indian cobra (the snake commonly used by snake charmers), and the coral snake, the only North American elapid.

Elapids are grouped together because of their similar way of killing their prey. They have hollow fangs at the front of the upper jaw. Instead of striking their prey like vipers and rattlesnakes, elapids chew into their prey with their fangs, which squeezes the venom into the muscles and body tissues. Mambas, in particular, have great speed and quick-acting venom, which can kill prey as large as a human being in ten minutes. Elapids eat primarily large mammals and other snakes.

Viperidae

One of the largest families of snakes is the Viperidae, or vipers. They live in many areas, including the Americas, Europe, Africa, Asia, and Australia. They have laterally placed eyes on triangular heads, a feature that gives them a wide range of vision as well as a distinctive appearance. Species from the family Viperidae include the gabboon viper and puff adder of Africa, the fer-de-lance of Central and South America, and the water moccasin of North America. These snakes all have hollow front fangs that fold up when the mouth is closed. Vipers strike at their prey, plunging their fangs into the animal's body and injecting venom into it. Depending on the species, a viper might eat

This Palestinian viper is an easily recognizable member of the viper family because of its triangular-shaped head and laterally placed eyes.

This Florida pine snake senses its surroundings with its tongue. The tongue is a vital sensory organ for snakes.

frogs, fish, turtles, rabbits, gophers, squirrels, and other small mammals.

The vipers that live in the Americas are called pit vipers—a group that includes water moccasins and rattlesnakes—because of the pits on their snouts that assist them in hunting prey. These facial pits sense heat as it radiates from living things. As this heat changes with the location and mass of the prey ahead of them, pit vipers can adjust their movements to track it.

Strong and unique sensory organs

Though snakes are numerous and their species varied, all of them share some characteristics that set them apart from other predators. For example, they all have unique and keen sensory organs, particularly when it comes to smell and hearing.

The tongue is the snake's most important sensory organ. It senses the animal's surroundings and the presence of food, enemies, or potential mates. Oddly enough, a snake does not use its tongue to taste. Instead, its tongue helps to feel the size and shape of objects around it. Primarily, however, a snake uses its tongue to sense odor by transferring chemical particles to a fluid-filled structure in its mouth called the Jacobson's organ. Nerve endings in the Jacobson's organ then interpret the chemical signals brought there by the tongue and direct this information to the brain.

In addition to its Jacobson's organ, a snake has a sense of smell similar to that of other animals for detecting more distant scents. It takes in these odors through its nasal passages by breathing air into areas called olfactory chambers. Cells in these chambers work in conjunction with the Jacobson's organ to translate the smells into nerve impulses, which are then sent to the brain.

Just as snakes do not smell or feel things in the same way that other animals do, the way they hear is unconventional as well. Snakes do not have external ears; rather, an inner ear structure allows them to receive vibrations that travel through the ground and into their bodies. Vibrations tell snakes if another creature is approaching, what size it is, and whether it is prey, enemy, or potential mate. Snakes also receive sound waves through their skin in the form of

Senses Used in Tandem

Snakes use a combination of touch, hearing, smell, and sight to locate and kill prey. In their book *Snakes in Question*, Carl H. Ernst and George R. Zug describe this ability.

A good example of the use of multiple senses is the ambushing technique of the timber rattlesnake . . . of eastern North America. The rattlesnake forages across the forest floor until it locates a rodent pathway by smell. The snake then follows the trail until it sees a suitable ambush site where the path runs along the top of a fallen log. Positioning itself beside the log, the rattlesnake rests its chin on the log, perpendicular to the path, and waits. When the mouse scurries onto the log, its arrival is detected by vibrations (hearing and touch). If there is sufficient light, the snake also sees the mouse with its eyes. As the mouse passes in front of the snake, the pit organs and eyes aim the strike. Contact with the mouse's body triggers the injection of venom and brief closure of the mouth around the mouse before the snake recoils. The mouse continues to run but soon collapses from the shock of envenomization. The rattlesnake uses smell, mainly from tongue flicks, to track and find the mouse.

vibrations that travel through their lungs to a bone in their jaw. From there, these vibrations are transferred into the ear bone, where they are finally transmitted to sound-sensitive cells in the inner ear.

Skin and scales

As its unique sensory organs allow it to hunt in very specific and successful ways, a snake's skin is uniquely adapted to its lifestyle. Every snake's body is covered with an elastic, scaly skin. A snake is able to exist in dry environments because it has two layers of skin, an inner layer called the dermis and a thinner layer on the outside called the epidermis. The dermis has blood vessels, nerve endings, glands, and connective tissues within it. The epidermis acts as armor and protects the snake's internal organs from punctures or scrapes. A snake's scales are produced by the epidermis and help maintain heat and water balance in the snake's body, regulate its exchange of gases, and form a barrier to microorganisms.

Because the epidermis must withstand all kinds of abuse, it wears out and must be replaced. Snakes accomplish this through a multiphased shedding process called ecdysis. In the early stage of the process, the bottom layer of the epidermis gradually produces new scales that will replace the old ones. As these new scales age, they die and become hard, thick, and full of keratin, the same material that the nails, hooves, and feathers of other animals are made of. At this point the scales are ready to become the snake's new outer layer. The outer sheath of older scales becomes soft and cloudy, including the snake's eye scales or spectacles. Because they cannot see to hunt or protect themselves until the old, cloudy eye scales are shed, snakes become nervous, hungry, and irritable just before shedding actually happens. Moreover, deprived of their normally keen eyesight, snakes are temporarily vulnerable to enemies. This explains why snakes often go into hiding during the roughly two-week period of shedding.

Ecdysis usually initiates around the lips, where a snake is able to rub its head against a rough surface of rock or bark. As the scaly skin catches on the rough surface, the snake crawls out of it. The skin is pulled off just as someone might pull off a sock. After shedding, the new epidermis is shiny and colorful.

The number of times a snake sheds per year depends on whether it is still growing and on the number of meals it has eaten. For example, a young snake will grow quite rapidly in its first year of life and will shed as many as a half dozen times per year; meanwhile a mature snake only sheds once a year, on average.

Feeding and growth

Though a snake does not have chewing teeth or claws with which to tear its prey, its body is uniquely adapted to swallowing its prey whole. In fact, considering its size, a snake is capable of eating some of the largest prey of any predatory animal thanks to several unique adaptations.

No matter what its age, a snake's elastic skin and unique rib cage allow it to easily swallow prey much larger than its body. Both layers of a snake's skin stretch and contract, allowing it to accommodate the passage of large meals through its digestive tract. Once the prey passes the snake's jaws, the neck and trunk muscles take over, contracting and moving the prey toward its stomach.

A ribbon snake swallows a goldfish. Swallowing prey whole is a unique characteristic of snakes.

Just as its scaly skin stretches to accommodate prey, the snake's jaw too has a unique structure that allows it to swallow large prey. A snake's jaw consists of several segmented bones connected by ligaments that allow these parts to move independently of one another. A pivot hinge in the back of the jaw also allows it to open wide enough to accommodate its prey. When a snake takes prey into its mouth, each of the bones in its upper and lower jaws moves independently. Naturalist Eric S. Grace explains this process: "Half of the jaw is always holding on, while the top half is loosened and moving forward to get a new hold. Bit by bit, the snake's jaws 'walk' their way over the prey which slowly disappears from sight."[2] After prey passes a snake's mouth, the snake readjusts its jawbones back into a resting position.

Though it would appear that a snake would not be able to breathe while swallowing an animal that completely fills its air passageway, the opening of its windpipe thrusts forward to the front of the snake's mouth so that it can still take air into its lungs. Snakes swallow their prey headfirst, pressing the body of their prey flatter and flatter so that it is easier to swallow and so that stray limbs will not catch in the snake's throat and cause choking.

Though a snake swallows its prey within ten to twenty minutes, digestion takes much longer. After swallowing its prey, the snake usually retreats to a safe place where it can lie still and digest its meal. The digestion process can take from a few days to weeks, depending on the size of the meal and on the temperature of the snake's body when it eats. When a snake is cold, the food digests more slowly than it does when its body is warmer.

Thermoregulation

The reason a snake's digestion is so subject to variation is because snakes are cold-blooded, meaning they do not maintain body temperature in the same way other warm-blooded animals do. Snakes are technically known as ectotherms, which means that the heat they need for survival comes from the outside rather than from metabolizing food. A snake regulates its body temperature by moving from shade to sun and

Snake Mysteries

In many ways, snakes continue to puzzle the humans who study them. In their book *Snakes in Question*, herpetologists Carl H. Ernst and George R. Zug describe a few of the things future researchers still have to learn about snakes.

Many aspects of the physiology of snakes remain poorly understood, including such critical processes as gas exchange through a reduced lung surface, blood pressure at various sites in the circulatory system, and the mechanism by which an adequate blood supply reaches the head when elevated. Processes involved in snakes' responses to temperature, including resistance to freezing during hibernation and the roles of temperature and hydration on sex determination (particularly in live-bearing snakes), remain unexplored. Finally, there is the intriguing question of why some snakes are immune to their own venom or that of other snakes and others are not.

back again, as needed. This process is called thermoregulation. In the early morning, for example, a snake may bask in the sun or in warm, shallow water when it is cold. Then, as its body warms, it moves into the shade again.

Since snakes do not need food to generate body heat, they may only eat two or three times a month on average to replenish the energy necessary for locomotion and other body functions. Because they do not need to eat often, snakes can live for long periods in deserts and other regions where food is scarce. Snakes can live in areas that experience seasonal drops in temperature, although they cannot live in places with consistently cold conditions because their bodies still need enough energy to enable them to hunt and reproduce.

Hibernation

Snakes can, however, survive surprisingly long periods of low temperature. In those areas where winter temperatures drop too low for snakes to maintain an adaquate body temperature, they hibernate. They must find a warm den, such as a burrow dug out by another animal or a fallen log, where they can safely become inactive. During hibernation, a snake's body temperature lowers, and it becomes dormant and neither eats nor burns energy. Temperature regulation remains vital, though, so snakes do move around in the den as needed to keep from freezing.

Snakes are not social animals, but some species will hibernate in groups because denning sites are not plentiful. Besides shelter, such communal dens provide snakes with opportunities for mating late in the hibernation season or immediately after, as the weather outside the den warms.

Mating and reproduction

Despite whether they have hibernated together, snakes meet to mate in the spring. A male finds a female by following a chemical scent produced in the female's body and secreted through her skin. Males also locate competing males by smelling odors released by scent glands in their backs. Regardless of species, the mating process in snakes is similar. During courtship, a male snake rubs its chin over the female's back. She then lifts her tail and aligns her cloacal vent with the male's. He inserts his reproductive organs inside her vent. Depending on the species of snake, mating can last from an hour to an entire day.

Snakes can either lay eggs or give birth to live young, depending on the species. Egg-laying snakes, including pythons, black racers, milk snakes, hognoses, and cobras, are known as oviparous. Oviparous snakes lay between 100 and 150 eggs at a time. Snake eggs must remain both warm and moist, so mother snakes look to make their nests in places like moist piles of leaves, compost piles, or inside rotting logs. In most snake species, the young hatch within six to twelve weeks. The baby snakes cut their way out of their shells by using a special egg tooth attached to the upper jaw. They lose this tooth within an hour or two after hatching.

Unlike their oviparous kin, viviparous snakes give birth to live offspring. After a gestation period of about twelve weeks, six to fifty snakes are born, still surrounded by a membranous coating. The baby snakes use their egg teeth to cut through this membrane.

Snake Locomotion

Though young and old snakes alike may seem particularly vulnerable because they do not have limbs with which to run away, snakes have adapted ways of moving quite quickly and efficiently. Most snakes use a movement called lateral undulation. They propel themselves in S curves, pushing against rocks, grass, or roots at the curve and moving themselves forward. Water-dwelling snakes use a swimming variation of lateral undulation to glide through the water, moving their oarlike tails in S curves to propel themselves.

Large, heavy snakes such as pythons and boas use a movement method called locomotion. The snake pushes forward in a straight line using its belly scales, or scutes. The scutes are attached to the snake's ribs, which are also attached to muscles that allow the scutes to move in groups, alternately touching the ground and moving the snake's body forward in waves.

Burrowing snakes and tree boas use accordion-like movements. Burrowing snakes use this motion to navigate through tunnels underground by alternately scrunching up and then expanding, thus pushing forward. Tree boas use the same technique to climb trees. They coil, push against a limb to brace themselves, then pull their tail up to meet their heads.

Though it has no limbs to use for locomotion, a snake's muscles and bones are uniquely constructed and connected to give it great range of movement and agility. A snake's skeleton is made up of a skull, backbone, and ribs. Snakes can have up to four hundred vertebrae, compared to thirty-three in people. Each of these vertebrae is jointed so the snake can move in multiple directions. Two ribs attach the spine to the skull, allowing the snake to turn its head. Muscles attach rib to rib, ribs to spinal column, vertebrae to vertebrae, and ribs to ventral scales. All of these attachments work to allow a snake great flexibility and coordination.

The basic skeleton of a snake consists of its skull, backbone, and ribs. Many muscles, which attach all of these bones to one another, allow snakes great coordination.

The necessity to keep snake eggs both warm and moist makes places like this hollow tree log ideal for a nest.

Whether viviparous or oviparous, mother snakes do not care for their young. Baby snakes are what is called precocial, meaning they can care for themselves immediately after birth or hatching. They start out eating worms or small insects like flies. Gradually, the young snakes eat larger prey, such as birds, small mammals, or toads. For the first year, however, these animals themselves may prey on the young snakes.

Snake defenses

To survive in an environment where they have many enemies and predators, snakes use their ability to move quickly in tandem with a variety of defense tools. The snake's first line of defense is to avoid a fight. As snake expert C. H. Pope says, "Snakes are first cowards, next bluffers, and last of all warriors."[3] A universal tool that snakes have to avoid being found is camouflage. They are often colored with patterns or blotches that match their surroundings, such as dead leaves. In addition to hiding them from enemies, camouflage helps hide them from prey they can catch by surprise.

While some snake species survive by staying hidden, others have evolved just the opposite strategy. Advertisement helps many poisonous snakes alert enemies to avoid them. For example, the brightly colored bands of the highly poisonous coral snake of the American South quickly turn enemies away.

So effective is advertisement that some snakes mimic poisonous snakes to discourage enemies. For instance, vipers are mimicked by some nonpoisonous snakes whose skin patterns, triangular head, and hissing and striking motions can fool an enemy into believing they are a dangerous viper. Herpetologists Carl H. Ernst and George R. Zug describe such mimicking behavior: "The toothless egg-eating snake *Dasypeltis scabra* of Africa not only matches the saw-scaled viper (*Echis carinatus*) in color, pattern and defensive behavior, but also creates the same rasping sound by rubbing together the scales in adjacent body loops."[4]

If camouflage, advertisement, or mimicry fails, then a snake will try to make noise that warns potential enemies. Though snakes do have vocal chords, they use other parts of their bodies to make sounds. Snakes hiss by filling their lungs and then rapidly contracting their bodies. Rattlesnakes of North America are named for the cone-shaped scales on the tail that interlock and rattle together when the snake whips its tail. Some snakes make popping sounds through their cloacal vent to startle predators. Others rustle their bodies in grass or leaves to alert another creature of their presence.

Many snakes use threatening behavior to repel an enemy, thus avoiding actual contact. For example, cobras spread their hoods to appear larger. Other snakes use even

The bright colored bands of the Arizona coral snake warn enemies of its highly poisonous nature and help deter advancing foes.

more dramatic displays. The West Indian ground boa squirts blood from its eyes to frighten a potential enemy. Eastern hognose snakes of North America puff up to appear larger, but if an enemy persists, they vomit up food, writhe on the ground, and then play dead by rolling over on their backs with their tongues hanging out.

If actually captured, many nonpoisonous snakes can constrict their musk glands and emit a foul-smelling odor to discourage an enemy. Garter snakes emit such a smell from their cloacal vent. Even some poisonous snakes make use of this strategy. Water moccasins spray such a scent by waving their tails about.

Venom

For 19 percent of the world's total population of snakes, an unavoidable confrontation will end in their biting an enemy and injecting venom from glands in their heads. Regardless of the species of snake it comes from, all venom is made of enzymes that digest the tissues around the area of the bite. In addition, venom may cause heart failure, prevent blood clotting, destroy blood cells, or damage the nervous systems of its victims. Though most snake bites are fatal for smaller animals, only about 100 of the 450 species of venomous snakes around the world have venom strong enough to cause serious problems for humans.

Cobras spread their hoods when confronted by an enemy in order to appear larger and more threatening.

Though snakes have many ways of protecting themselves, they face a variety of threats that they cannot avoid, such as humans who kill them outright or collect them from the wild to supply the commercial market. However, the predominant threat to the current and future survival of snakes worldwide is habitat destruction as more and more land is appropriated by human beings for agriculture or other kinds of development.

2

Dwindling Snake Habitat

AROUND THE WORLD, habitat for snakes is eroding. Sometimes habitat is destroyed outright to make way for human dwellings or industry. Other times, habitat is contaminated by pesticides or snakes are crowded out by the introduction of exotic animal species. Regardless of the source of habitat loss, the result is always the same: snake populations decline as a result. Biologists were slow to notice the decline in snake numbers, but as early as 1975 biologist Robert H. Mount expressed concern for the survival of some snake species: "Much of the detrimental habitat manipulation is the result of the increasing human population and its demands on the natural environment. Extensive land clearing, whether for housing, industry, mineral exploration or agriculture, takes a heavy toll."[5] In the United States, more than half of the snake species currently listed as endangered have declined as a direct result of habitat destruction.

Altered wetland and coastal habitats

Snakes that depend on wetlands, streams, or unique coastal habitats cannot live just anyplace but depend on areas with the unique conditions necessary for their survival. Human alteration of such areas to create agricultural fields or housing developments has taken a heavy toll on many snake species around the world.

For instance, some snakes, such as the gulf salt marsh snake and the Atlantic salt marsh snake, have become increasingly threatened with the dwindling of their highly specialized habitat, marshes and swamps located near where rivers empty into the ocean. Unlike snakes that can live in freshwater, these snakes have adapted to life in a primarily saltwater environment. Developers who drain marshes to make room for homesites near the ocean threaten them with extinction.

The copperbelly water snake of the American Midwest also requires very specific and increasingly rare wetland habitat. Though in the winter they hibernate in dry upland areas and spend much of the late summer and fall in woodland areas, copperbelly water snakes spend a few crucial months of the spring and early summer in woodland swamps, which provide them a place to mate and find their prey, which consists of frogs, tadpoles, and fish. Originally, conversion of wetland habitat to agricultural areas reduced the snake's numbers. But since the mid-1980s, the greater danger to the snake is modifications of its habitat such as dredging, coal mining, stream channelization, and road construction, in addition to commercial and residential development. The increased sedimentation associated with residential construction also fills in the snake's remaining wetland habitat, choking out the vegetative cover that the snake hides in and killing off the populations of amphibians and fish that the snake relies on for food.

The gulf salt marsh snake lives in a very specific habitat that when destroyed or altered leads to their decline.

Copperbelly water snakes represent a kind of indicator species that signals humans about the health of the entire wetland ecosystem. As a predator, the copperbelly lives at the top of the food chain and acts as a gauge of the health of the whole ecosystem it inhabits. If the copperbelly is in trouble, then chances are the entire wetland ecosystem is in trouble as well.

Agriculture takes its toll

Agriculture and livestock grazing have also taken a heavy toll on snakes. Around the world, large tracts of land have been cleared, burned, plowed, and mowed, leaving many snakes with radically altered habitats. In many countries, fires are set to promote growth of grazing vegetation for vast herds of domestic animals. The fires have either killed snakes outright or left them without adequate prey or vegetative cover. For example, on the Indian Ocean island of Madagascar, the Madagascar ground boa annually loses more acres of its already limited habitat to such controlled fires. The species has been listed as endangered since 1977.

Though sometimes snake species can adapt to such altered habitats, rarely are they able to thrive there. Massasauga rattlesnakes are one good example of the problem. They are barely holding on in the southwestern United States because their grassland habitat has been converted to agricultural use. In some areas, overgrazing has caused mesquite thickets to grow unchecked, choking out native grasses needed by the massasaugas as cover. Because their vegetative habitat has been largely destroyed, massasaugas have had to adapt to living in the dens of banner-tailed kangaroo rats, themselves an endangered species. The dens represent a microhabitat that changes little in temperature from season to season and affords them plentiful pocket mice, lizards, and giant centipedes that enter the holes. Conservationists hope that if the kangaroo rats and their habitat can be protected, the massasauga will benefit as a result.

Unmanaged forestry: a problem for snakes

Forest destruction, whether to promote agriculture or for logging, can cause a number of problems for snake species,

Improper Management of Refuges

Even in some areas set aside for conservation purposes, snake species have declined further as a result of improper management. For example, the prairie garter snake, an endangered species in Ohio, has been further threatened by improper game management practices. When game management officials increased the number of ponds in the refuge to attract Canadian geese, the prairie garter also found the marshy prairie habitat exactly suited to its own survival. Unfortunately, officials mowed extensively around the ponds so that the geese could easily forage for seed and grains in those areas. The extensive mowing killed many snakes attracted to the area. George H. Dalrymple and Norman G. Reichenbach conducted a study at the site and reported in their *Biological Conservation* article "Management of an Endangered Species of Snake in Ohio, USA," that "on four trips to our study site following mowing operations, a total of 39 dead snakes were found, 17 of which were *T. radix* [prairie garter snake]."

Even while living in special conservation areas, the prairie garter snake's numbers dropped due to poor management of these areas.

The results of the study indicate that wildlife officials must change their management approach if the endangered prairie garter is to survive in one of its last remaining Ohio habitats. Dalrymple and Reichenbach recommended that the site be mowed but during daily and seasonal times when the snakes are not as active and retreat to their dens.

the most serious one being loss of populations with adequate genetic diversity. Forest destruction results in the long-term problem of what herpetologist Kenneth Dodd calls "the fragmentation of remaining population size and the resulting potential loss of genetic diversity."[6] As habitats are fragmented by logging, potential breeding snakes are unable able to reach each other. As the available number of breeding snakes grows smaller and more isolated, inbreeding can

The destruction of trees in a snake's habitat can have severe consequences for the species, including breeding decline and inbreeding.

occur, resulting in offspring with deformities, lower resistance to disease, and myriad other genetic problems. One suggested solution to this problem of habitat fragmentation has been to preserve habitat corridors connecting the otherwise isolated patches of forest, theoretically allowing for movement from one protected area to another. However, herpetologists such as Dodd argue that snakes "will not likely abandon preferred habitats to move between isolated habitat patches."[7]

Other snakes are dependent on the trees themselves. For example, the Round Island keel-scaled boa, an arboreal snake, relies on the trees for both resting and hunting. Also, the trees protect it from attack by predatory mammals. These snakes must come down to the ground to mate, and without the cover of surrounding trees and dead and decaying trees on the forest floor, they are vulnerable to predation by other animals as well as attack or capture by humans.

Many snakes depend on trees for protection from the scorching heat of the sun. In India, for instance, massive cutting of the scrub forest in favor of agriculture has caused the Indian python to decline in huge numbers. Not only has the destruction of the scrub forest reduced the populations of the python's small tree-dwelling mammal prey, it has also left the snake without shade trees for taking refuge during the hottest part of the day.

Sometimes, well-meaning efforts at conservation can be harmful if not carefully planned. The threatened broad-headed snake of Australia depends on gray gum trees in the heavily logged forests adjacent to its rocky habitat on the sandstone plateaus from Newcastle to Nowra. During the hot Australian summers, the snake moves away from its typical habitat of sandstone outcroppings into the woodlands, where it seeks out large gray gum trees with hollows in their trunks. Researchers have collected evidence from people who have seen the snakes migrate from the rocks to the trees and have also tracked the snakes using radio telemetry to confirm that they indeed depend on such tree hollows. The standard forestry practice of removing dead or overly mature trees, the ones likely to have the hollows that the snakes prefer, is diminishing summer habitat for the snakes. The study revealed that forestry practices have indeed impacted the broad-headed snake. Scientists have determined that foresters need to leave many such habitat trees in the forest, especially those nearest the snake's rocky habitat. As biologists Jonathan K. Webb and Richard Shine report, current forest management plans do not call for leaving such trees and that "forestry activities are likely to have a negative impact on broad-headed snake populations either because too few habitat trees are retained . . . or because habitat trees are clumped or inappropriately located."[8]

Deforestation in the natural habitat of the Indian python has left it with fewer tree animals to prey on and without shade.

Human developments consume snake habitats

Human residential developments also destroy habitat needed by snakes such as the broad-headed snake of Australia. In the winter months, the broad-headed snake leaves its roosts and inhabits sandstone outcroppings near Sydney. Researchers concerned by the drop in numbers of the broad-headed snake have determined that removal of bush rocks from the outcroppings for use in decorative gardens has caused the snake's population to decline. Researchers say that, given that, bush-rock collectors remove the same types of rocks . . . as those used by the snakes and their primary prey, and that snake and lizard densities are apparently controlled by rock availability, the implications are clear. Unless the activities of bush-rock collectors can be curtailed, the considerable range reduction experienced by the broad-headed snake is likely to continue.[9]

Sometimes the problem is not that humans remove resources from snakes' habitats, but that they want to live in the areas that were formerly ideal snake habitats. In many

Multiple Threats to the Habitat of the Kirtland's Snake

Some snake species are adversely impacted by not just one but several types of human activity. This means that even if one threat is addressed, the others may continue to endanger the species. The threatened Kirtland's snake of the American Midwest is just such a snake. It requires a specific and increasingly imperiled wetland habitat made up of wet prairies, meadows, and prairie fens that humans have drained to convert the land to agricultural fields. Though the Kirtland's snake has adapted somewhat to its drier habitat, it must live in crawfish burrows in the vicinity of a pond, lake, or creek area prone to seasonal flooding. Most of the population has been isolated into low grassy areas along creeks, ponds, and ditches, and some have even been isolated in the midst of housing developments where they will inevitably decline due to lack of suitable den sites.

Even if part of the snake's wetland habitat remains intact, it faces other dangers as well. A survey in Illinois revealed that controlled fires, automobile traffic, field and roadside mowing, and herbicides sprayed in railroad rights-of-way have also caused the Kirtland's snake to decline.

The Kirtland's snake remains threatened not only from immediate destruction of its habitat but from other human activity like controlled fires, herbicides, field mowing, and even traffic.

countries around the world, the story is much the same for species living in areas desired for human development. The Jamaican boa represents a good example of the effects residential developments can have on a species. The snake is being hedged into a smaller and smaller territory as its habitat is altered by human residential developments. By the end of the twentieth century, it had been confined to a small fraction of its former territory on the island. Now, even that territory is being destroyed to make way for a rapidly increasing human population drawn to the beautiful island. In order to survive, this large, striking, silver-gray snake has changed its diet from birds and mammals it found in the wild to those creatures that thrive in residential gardens such as rats and mice. But even this food source is not completely reliable, since residents have begun to use rodenticides to control the populations of these rodents.

Similarly, the southern United States, an area once rich with a diversity of snake species, is being developed so quickly that many species are dwindling in number. For example, the rim rock crowned snake of southeast Florida is in danger of extinction as a result of residential and commercial development of its habitat. Conservationists hope that it might stand a chance with, as herpetologist Paul E. Moler says, "the incorporation of environmental considerations into open space design, public parks, and green belts along highways and throughout low-density residential developments."[10] Also, the eastern indigo snake, which lives in southern states such as Florida and Alabama, requires large tracts of unbroken habitat. To find enough prey to eat, a single eastern indigo snake requires as much as a twenty-five-hundred-acre plot of land where it is free to move about. Rapid housing development and road construction have made this impossible for many indigo snakes.

Roads designed to move an increasing number of people to and from their jobs and homes also have a devastating effect on snakes. Such roads cut through habitat, and as snakes move about in their territory, they are often killed by vehicular traffic.

A gopher snake lies across a road that cuts through the eastern Sierra Nevada mountains in California. Many snakes die from traffic when roads cut through their natural habitat.

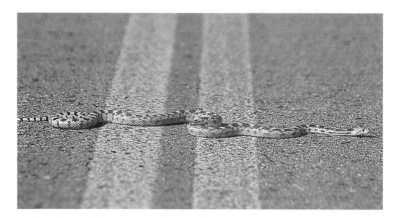

Such traffic is a particularly severe problem for snakes in the United States. For instance, on "one 44-km stretch of roadway in southern Arizona, traffic kills between 500 and 1,000 snakes each year."[11] A study of highways that pass through the Organ Pipe Cactus National Monument in southern Arizona uncovered numerous road-killed snakes. Among the 368 dead snakes counted were representatives of two snake species, the *Chionactis palarostris* and *Lichanura trivirgata trivirgata*, species so rare that they cannot be found anywhere else in the United States.

Exotic species threaten snakes

Besides the outright destruction of habitat, the introduction of exotic species can render otherwise suitable habitat useless to some snakes. Fire ants, introduced to the southern United States, are just one example of an exotic species—that is, a species not native to the region. Accidentally brought to the United States from South America, fire ants have established colonies throughout the South, as far north as Virginia and as far west as California. The fire ants do not attack adult snakes; instead, they wait until the eggs of oviparous snakes begin to hatch and then enter the shell and eat the young snake. Eckerd College professor Elizabeth Forys discovered in a study financed by the Florida Fish and Wildlife Conservation Commission that the spread of fire ants is aided by development. She says, "In the really pristine areas, there were not any fire ants. . . . Our hypothesis is they prefer disturbed areas because there are fewer native ants there—no competitors."[12]

In Australia, the Caribbean, Europe, and many other places, too, such exotic species have threatened the survival of some snakes and caused still others to become extinct. Exotic species can cause untold damage to the existing balance of predator and prey already in the area. Feral, or wild, cats, rats, or even goats often take hold in a snake's habitat, either killing the snake for food or breaking down, consuming, or otherwise contaminating its habitat. For example, a nonnative toad introduced into Australia is poisonous, and countless native snakes have died after eating it. Another example is the mongoose, a small, slender mammal native to India and known to prey on snakes, that was introduced by humans to protect them from venomous snakes found on the islands of the Caribbean. The mongoose has thrived, directly causing the decline of several snake species.

 ## Island Species Are at Special Risk

The smaller the geographic area over which a species is distributed, the more prone it is to extinction. Consequently, island snake species are extremely vulnerable. Many conservationists have made it a priority to determine the populations of these endangered island species and their habitat requirements to better understand how to protect them. Isolated patches of habitat may sustain populations for a time, but eventually genetic inbreeding will cause them to decline and die off.

Island species also allow scientists to better understand how extinction occurs and to learn what steps can be taken to prevent it. By studying island snake species, scientists have already discovered some hopeful information about their rate of extinction. In their *American Naturalist* article "Reptile Extinctions on Land-Bridge Islands: Life-History Attributes and Vulnerability to Extinction," writers Johannes Foufopoulos and Anthony R. Ives say, "The rate of species loss varies greatly and depends on island size, time since isolation, and taxa [species] examined. Past studies have shown that larger islands lose species at a slower rate and that bird or mammal taxa are more susceptible to extinction than are reptiles."

The mongoose, an animal once restricted to India, is at fault for drastically lowering snake populations in the Caribbean.

One species of island boa, the Round Island boa, has been harmed indirectly by introduction of exotic species. Nonnative sheep, goats, and pigs introduced into this snake's island home in the Indian Ocean eat too much of the vegetative cover necessary for the snake to forage and breed in. This shy snake, which lives in holes in crumbly earth, is also endangered even by rabbits, who eat tree seedlings, which contributes to deforestation. To offset these harmful effects, conservationists are replanting damaged areas of forests and attempting to control the populations of these nonnative species.

Similarly, the primary problems facing the Virgin Islands boa are the huge populations of mongoose, rats, and feral cats roaming over its tiny island habitat. Though the small uninhabited cays and islets that are part of the Virgin Islands ecosystem provide protection from these exotic predators and from humans, the snakes living on these tiny bits of land are vulnerable to severe ocean storms. Conservationists hope that their aggressive rat eradication programs on the larger islands will provide more habitat for this seriously endangered snake.

Pesticides affect snake species

Though their effects are not as easily identified or controlled as those of exotic species, pesticides have also had detrimental effects on snake species. Aside from killing snakes directly, these chemicals can cause a number of other problems for snakes, including causing snake eggs to be too delicate, causing deformities in young snakes, and killing off a snake's prey animals or contaminating that prey so that the snake is then poisoned by its food. Herpetologist Robert H. Mount describes the subtlety of the pesticide problem:

It is reasonable to assume that the effects vary widely with the pollutant as well as with the species. Some forms not killed outright by a harmful chemical may be affected adversely in subtle ways. Reproductive functions may be impacted, or the chemical may reach toxic levels through bioaccumulation. Some pollutants may not affect a reptile or amphibian directly, but may reduce or eliminate its food supply. It is not unlikely that environmental contaminants are responsible for many of the cases in which certain species are declining when other adverse factors are not apparent.[13]

Though the effects of pesticides on mammal and bird populations have been widely documented, the effects on reptiles are only now being investigated and discussed by scientists. One reason may be that snakes are, due to their secretive nature, not readily observed. Moreover, the effects of pesticides are usually not obvious in snakes.

In a few cases, however, the connection between pesticides and snake deaths are fairly clear-cut. Dieldrin, a pesticide sprayed in Africa to control the tsetse fly that spreads sleeping sickness, has directly killed many snakes. A study revealed that Mirex, a chemical used to control fire ants—ironically, an exotic species harmful to oviparous snakes—remains in snake tissue for eighteen months, causes the snake's health to decline, and makes it difficult for it to produce viable eggs and healthy young. One study suggests a link between pesticides and declining snake populations. In two adjacent river valleys in southern Texas, one treated with agricultural pesticides and the other left untreated, researchers noted a clear difference. Herpetologist Harry W. Greene says that the untreated valley "harbors a typical snake fauna, while the second lacks ratsnakes and other egg-laying species; given their proven effects on reproduction in other vertebrates, a reasonable guess is that pesticides eliminated those Texas snakes."[14]

The dangers for snakes go beyond habitat loss, however. Even if endangered snake habitat is preserved and protected from contaminants, snakes still face the danger of people who continue to seek out and kill them out of fear or to sell them as food or leather to domestic and international markets.

3

Direct Killing of Snakes

THE FEAR AND dislike of snakes have a long history. Even Benjamin Franklin referred to rattlesnakes as "felons . . . from the Beginning of the World."[15] Annually, hundreds of thousands of snakes are killed by humans. Some are killed for sport, some for their skins or meat, and a significant number die simply because the people who live around them kill them out of irrational fear. Given the frequency and, in most cases, widespread condoning of the practice, the killing presents a very real threat to many threatened and endangered snake species worldwide.

To supply the seemingly endless demand for snakeskin products, such as belts, shoes, and other leather goods, hunters kill a substantial number of snakes each year. Most skins are exported from South America, Africa, and Asia, particularly China, Hong Kong, Singapore, and Indonesia. Dealers do not have to look very hard for willing buyers. In Great Britain, statistics show that in the year 1992 alone, 230,000 snakeskins were imported. Worldwide, the highest demand for imported snakeskins comes from Japan, the United States, and from the wealthy countries of Europe. The impact of this commerce on snake populations worries biologists. Herpetologist Chris Mattison says, "It is difficult to see how snake populations can continue to sustain trade of this magnitude."[16]

Perhaps not surprisingly, snakes with brightly colored and uniquely patterned skins draw the highest prices. The most popular species are the threatened reticulated python and the endangered Indian python. Also popular are giant and yellow anacondas, which are sold in huge numbers to the United States from markets in Argentina, Bolivia, Panama, and Peru. Worldwide, one hundred thousand boa constrictor skins are sold each year. The Java file snake and the Indian rat snake are also heavily traded.

Snake hunters even go into the world's oceans in search of their quarry. Asian marine snakes affected by the leather market are the Javanese *Acrochordidae* snake and the *A. granulatus*. Also, marine snakes off the coast of Gata Island

A model poses in a snakeskin-patterned outfit. The intricate design of snakeskin has made it a favorite in the fashion world and many snakes are killed each year for their skin.

in the Philippines have been overharvested to such an extent that populations in the area are now threatened. Many of the hunters are poor people who see hunting sea snakes as a way to make a living, even though most of these hunters receive only a small fraction of the price the final products made from the skins fetch. As herpetologist Jean Lescure says, marine snakes are "sold to local tanneries, often for a ridiculously low sum."[17]

Even so-called common species of snakes have been affected by the skin trade. Lescure points out that, "as is the case with most wildlife trade, the most expensive species are targeted, but as they are usually protected or extinct, often related and cheaper species take their place. Many small pythons and boas, like the Asian blood python, are now pressured by the market. . . . This snake is now seriously endangered by overexploitation."[18] Though also once considered a common species, the timber rattlesnake, which is native to the United States, declined in large part because of its demand on the commercial market. Though a much less familiar sight in the wild, timber rattler skin is still a common sight on hat bands, belts, and boots.

Because of the trade in skins, the populations of many species have dropped to the point that some countries are concerned about their survival. For instance, India and Sri Lanka, two countries that are home to a great number of sought-after species, have expressed concern about the detrimental effects of the snake skin trade. To stem the tide of collection and killing, these nations now strictly regulate all exports of snakeskin. India now allows "only for the sale of finished products, and these under government regulation."[19]

Despite regulations under terms of an international treaty known as the Convention on International Trade in Endangered Species of Wild Flora and Fauna (CITES), traffic in snakeskins is difficult to regulate because skins can be imported as pieces or whole. As a result, officials cannot verify the actual number of snakes that were killed to produce a shipment of skins. In the case of finished products, some snakes may not be counted at all, and others may be

Snakes as Food

Though not as widespread as the desire for snakeskins, a taste for snake meat also brings a steady flow of business to vendors in many cultures. People in a number of Asian countries eat snake on a regular basis. The trade in snake products is particularly vigorous in the large Asian cities of Hong Kong, Canton, and Shanghai, where pythons, cobras, and sea kraits prepared for human consumption are common sights in markets. In his book *Encyclopedia of Snakes,* writer and snake expert Chris Mattison says that in most countries, the effects of such consumption are "thought to be minor, other than in China, where tens of thousands of snakes are eaten each year."

Though in some cultures eating snakes is considered taboo, elsewhere people kill and eat snakes they encounter in the wild even though they provide considerably less flesh than other animals. Snakes are easily caught and can provide supplements to diets in areas where other prey animals may have become scarce or difficult to locate. For example, when other prey animals are not readily available, the bushmen of South Africa eat the large boid snakes found in their region. Mattison says that Australian aborigines also "eat all varieties of snakes and relish pythons in particular. In parts of tropical Africa the rock python is held in high esteem and anacondas and common boas are eaten in South America." Cambodian fishermen will eat water snakes found in nets, though they do not intentionally set out specifically to catch them.

counted too many times because a single snake skin can be turned into one or more products. Also, though CITES requires snakeskin shipments to list the country of origin because a snake may be more endangered in one area than another, this term *country of origin* is often interpreted so loosely by shippers as to be of little value. Herpetologist Kenneth Dodd says that "it is not uncommon to encounter *Boa* products imported from the Far East, or to see thousands of python skins with their country of origin listed as Singapore or Europe."[20]

For customs officials trying to enforce CITES regulations, the task of verifying whether skins being shipped come from an endangered species is immense. Denise Sewell, writer for *E* magazine, reported what she saw at a warehouse of suspect animal products confiscated at ports of entry by U.S. Fish and Wildlife officials and given to laboratory workers trained in identifying the species that products have come from: "There are rows and rows of boots, some with cobra heads, others fashioned with the skins of python."[21] Though advanced computer programs are currently being developed that could quickly identify which species a snakeskin product has come from, these programs are not yet ready for general use.

Because customs officials are at such a disadvantage, CITES has not been effective in controlling even blatantly illegal trade. Moreover, deceptive practices mean that some contraband will slip by inspectors. A brisk trade still goes on even in skins taken from endangered species because traffickers, as Jean Lescure says, "are always devising new strategies to transport skins, sometimes going so far as to counterfeit customs documents."[22]

Snakes used in traditional medicine

In addition to their skins, snakes are often killed for other body parts. In some cultures, people kill endangered snakes to use their parts in traditional medicine. In some parts of China, for example, the gallbladders of snakes are believed to be of powerful medicinal benefit. Humans consume a huge number of snake parts in the mistaken belief that they function as cures for sickness and as aphrodisiacs. Herpetologists Carl H. Ernst and George R. Zug disparage such practices, saying, "The effectiveness of snake parts for curing various illnesses is highly questionable, as is their use as aphrodisiacs or virility boosters."[23] Despite such scientific opinions about the ineffectiveness of snake parts as medicine, Asian liquor companies still capture the threatened short-tailed mamushi snake and insert it into bottles of high-priced whiskey. The liquor is said to improve people's skin and lengthen their lives. Also, in Maharashtra, a region in west central India, the residents believe that oil from the fat of the seriously endangered Indian python can cure arthritis, and so they collect and kill the snake despite laws protecting the species.

Fear of bites

Sometimes people kill snakes not for their skin or body parts but to protect themselves and their families from the dangers—real or imagined—that snakes pose. Indisputably, many snakes in South America, Africa, and Asia have the ability to bite and, in some cases, kill human beings. Where they are perceived to present a threat to humans, snakes are killed in large numbers. For example, each year great numbers of terciopelos and bushmasters, two highly venomous pit vipers that inhabit the tropical forests and fields from Mexico to South America, are killed by local people. Such killing is for the most part needless, however. According to herpetologist Harry W. Greene, neither species is as aggressive as many people

Despite its rather non-aggressive nature, the highly venomous Costa Rican bushmaster is often killed because people perceive it as a threat.

believe. In fact, both snakes "avoid contact with humans . . . [and] remained still or glided off when we approached them closely."[24] The proper clothing and an awareness and understanding of the habits and habitats of venomous snakes can, at least in part, protect people from attack.

The Fiji snake, too, a small, dark brown, extremely venomous elapid that lives in the burrows of mammals and under stones and rotting logs on this Pacific island, is a target of humans who are afraid of its bite. Its venom is neurotoxic, meaning that it affects the central nervous system of anything it bites, and is almost always deadly to humans. Based on unofficial reports from locals, herpetologists have surmised that its numbers have dropped mainly because of killing by local people afraid of being bitten.

Though snakes can and do kill humans, nearly 40 percent of the bites inflicted on humans each year by venomous snakes, even those of highly feared tropical species, are actually "dry"—that is, bites in which the snake does not inject any venom. According to *Smithsonian* writer Scott Weidensaul, "Of the nearly 8,000 venomous snake bites each year in the United States, only a dozen or so result in death—in part because a large percentage of bites are 'dry.'"[25]

Moreover, snake bites are quite rare. Weidensaul points out that rattlesnakes only bite if provoked to the point that they feel their life is threatened. He cites one particular example of a fellow researcher who was trying to locate a specific male rattlesnake included in a research project:

> The yellow-phase snake, cryptic against the dead oak leaves, was curled within six inches of her boot. It never moved, never rattled, never made the slightest sign of anger or alarm. Later in the day, we all unwittingly walked within two feet of a thick 45-incher that didn't stir a muscle in protest, even when [herpetologist Howard] Reinert knelt beside it to slide a thermometer next to its coils.[26]

Misinformation feeds fear

Many threatened snakes, even harmless, nonpoisonous species, die at the hands of misinformed people who see

All Snakes Are Not Alike

Renowned herpetologist Archie Carr spent his life trying to educate people about snakes and their habitats. As
the following excerpt from his essay "Black Water,
Green Light" in editor Les Line's anthology *What We Save Now* illustrates, because of people's innate fear and dislike of snakes, he
was not always a successful educator.

> I told [a local fisherman] I had seen only one moccasin there, and that
> one away back in March; but he said that hell, all them snakes swimming
> around out there back and forth across the lake was moccasins. "There is
> days they about ruin the place," he said. . . . On a misguided impulse I
> picked up my snake bag and took out the snake I had there . . . and the
> man said godalmighty and went up to his pickup and drove away. . . . I
> stood there with mixed feelings, sorry I had offended him, but at the same
> time pondering that water snakes are a two-edged sword in a way, be-
> cause they both help to save wet
> country from invasion, by scaring
> people off to safer sites of outdoor
> recreation; and give heart to mindless
> or mercenary men who call swamps
> useless places, or fetid quagmires rife
> with venomous snakes and disease-
> carrying mosquitoes, and so persuade
> the public to let them dig canals. . . .
> And if snakes are not admissible evi-
> dence of the value of wilderness, then
> they at least shouldn't count as
> grounds for wrecking it.

*People tend to have unreasonable
fears of snakes, such as this
cottonmouth water moccasin,
because they have a lack of
knowledge of them.*

them as dangerous. For example, in India, illegal killing of
the seriously endangered Indian python continues even
though, if prosecuted, people face a year in jail. Herpetologist Romulus Whitaker reports that he "interviewed a tribal
hunter near Madras who claims he killed at least 80 individuals of *P. molurus* [the Indian python] in the past three
years."[27] Whitaker says that "outside of protected reserves,
P. molurus survival in India is becoming increasingly dubi-
ous . . . in general because large predators (and particularly
large snakes) are not tolerated by humans."[28] Herpetologists

The harmless milk snake (pictured) often is killed because its brightly colored bands give it the appearance of the highly venomous coral snake.

have difficulty convincing local people that the Indian python serves a very useful role in rodent control.

Sometimes people kill and endanger the populations of even harmless snakes because they cannot distinguish them from poisonous species. For instance, the eastern indigo snake has declined in its habitat in Florida and Georgia partly because people unfamiliar with it have killed it because they cannot distinguish it from poisonous species it resembles. Also, harmless milk snakes are often killed because they closely resemble the highly poisonous coral snake with its alternating bands of yellow, black, and red.

Evidence suggests that humans killing a snake species can directly cause its decline. Greene says that more than half of all pit viper species and, specifically, a third of rattlesnake pit viper species have been brought to the edge of extinction by fearful people. He says the rattlesnake's "salvation ultimately depends on changes in our attitudes toward snakes, and that is a matter of education."[29] In the northeastern United States, the timber rattlesnake, an especially misunderstood and endangered pit viper, is nearly extinct because of killing by humans. As a result, there have been calls to put this snake on the federal endangered species list. Biologists can only try to halt the decline.

They cannot reintroduce the snake to its former habitat because many residents of the states where the species is now extinct protest the snake's reintroduction.

Bounties and roundups

Sometimes the killing of snakes continues because the practice has become part of local tradition. For decades timber and other rattlesnakes have been legally hunted in organized events called roundups. Once organized to remove rattlesnakes from populated areas, the events continue in some states today despite having accomplished the original goal decades ago. Until very recently many state agencies approved of the hunts and even offered bounties for hides from rattlesnakes.

During a roundup, people use a variety of tools to capture and/or kill the snakes. Participants have used poles tipped with fish hooks to pull the snakes from their dens. Some people also put road flares or pour gasoline into the dens to drive rattlesnakes into the open, where they can collect them. The

The western diamondback rattlesnake population has dwindled because of organized roundups in which these snakes are killed or captured in great numbers.

Rattlesnake Education

Author and herpetologist Harry W. Greene found a rattlesnake basking on a wall at a Berkeley, California, day-care center that he visits in an effort to teach children about nature. While the children watched, Greene moved the snake to safety. Each year, he talks about this particular rattlesnake at the day-care center, reminding the children that it is probably still nearby and that they have very little to fear if they watch out for and respect it. In his book *Snakes: The Evolution of Mystery in Nature*, Greene expresses the role he and this snake have played in trying to teach children to respect rather than fear rattlesnakes: "Prejudices evaporate as my students come to see rattlesnakes as an accumulation of special adaptations to their environment. . . . If we have a rational perspective on the role of rattlers in natural ecosystems and their threat to humans, finding one can be as precious as seeing a wildcat or a raptor."

captured rattlesnakes are eventually killed and sold for their meat or skins, but many are kept for months without food or water. Crowded into containers, the captives often crush or bite each other to death. The Humane Society of the United States states, "Investigators have seen snakes being dropped onto concrete floors from crates several feet above the ground, putted with golf clubs while in a coiled position."[30] People also have used dynamite, crowbars, and hydraulic truck jacks to destroy the rocky dens of snakes during the hunts. Many gravid (egg-laden) females are killed in a roundup because they are often easily found on exposed basking sites. The killing of female snakes is particularly destructive since more females than males are necessary if a rattlesnake population is to remain large and healthy.

Once chased from their dens, some rattlesnakes are killed outright. Though rattlesnakes are not necessarily killed during a roundup, most eventually die as a result of the disturbance. Most are highly sensitive, and many die simply from the stress of being captured. Even snakes that survive capture and are subsequently released do not survive. They are released by roundup participants into territories they are unfamiliar with and to which they cannot adapt because they rely on using the same den year after year. As Weidensaul explains,

> Grown rattlers moved far from their home territory may simply wander in circles for months until they freeze, even though local dens are available. Apparently just any old den won't do; it must be their den, the one they've used since infancy, and recent genetic work suggests that the snakes in each den form something of an extended family, rather than a random sample of local rattlesnakes.[31]

Advocates of rattlesnake roundups defend them by saying that they are a means of collecting venom, which is used to make antivenin, the antidote to rattlesnake bites. However, this defense simply does not hold up. U.S. producers of anitivenins are regulated by strict Food and Drug Administration guidelines, which prohibit use of venom collected during roundups because venom degrades rapidly when exposed to air, and without the proper storage facilities, roundup organizers cannot prevent such exposure.

Despite the cruelty that often goes along with such events, rattlesnake roundups go on legally in many states. Local authorities are often reluctant to end the traditional events even when local sentiment turns against them. For example, when faced with a seven-hundred-signature petition calling for the end of the local roundup—now in its thirty-third year—the mayor of Claxton, Georgia, told *Savannah Morning News* reporter Anne Cordeiro that the roundup "will continue unless there is a state or federal law that prohibits it."[32]

As a result of such attitudes, many ancestral rattlesnake dens are destroyed and their inhabitants killed each year, frustrating the efforts of herpetologists to study the snakes. For this reason, herpetologists are extremely secretive about den sites where they study snakes such as the belled viper, a subspecies of the timber rattlesnake. As a result of repeated attacks on dens, the belled viper is now endangered in ten states. Weidensaul says that while researching an article about the belled viper, he was "sworn to secrecy by many snake hunters and researchers, threatened with blindfolds . . . and admonished with stories about sites that were cleaned out by poachers because someone had a loose tongue."[33]

In some cases, it does not take organized roundups to seriously endanger a snake species. In Greece, populations of the threatened Lebetine viper have similarly dwindled to dangerously low numbers because of bounties once offered by the government. This snake is known only to exist on the islands of Milos, Kimilos, Polinos, Siphnos, and Kythonos, located in the Mediterranean near the Greek mainland. The largest viper in Europe, the Lebetine viper lives in dense vegetation broken by areas where it can sun itself. In search of these basking areas, it often comes close to agricultural areas, where it comes into contact with residents who fear and kill it.

Nonpoisonous snakes are killed in roundups

In killing campaigns and roundups, many nonpoisonous species of snakes are killed in the process. For instance, during campaigns to kill the Lebetine viper, the threatened Aegean water snake and other species of snakes are often killed by nondiscriminating hunters. Similarly, hunters of the endangered eastern diamondback rattlesnakes often kill other endangered snakes, such as the Florida pine snake and eastern indigo snake, whose habitats overlap that of the rattler. All three species may use abandoned gopher tortoise burrows as dens. In roundups to kill the eastern diamondback, hunters pour gasoline into the dens, killing all three snakes in the process. In fact, the eastern indigo snake is now extinct in Alabama due in large part to the rattlesnake roundups.

Not all snake hunters fear snakes or even mean them direct harm. Many people purposely set out to collect snakes to keep them in captivity. Some people keep these snakes as pets or sell them to the burgeoning pet trade around the world. Others hunt for endangered snakes in the wild so that they can collect and breed them in captivity. The danger to the snakes, though, is no less real.

4

The Complications of Collection

NOT ALL PEOPLE fear snakes or see them as sources of skins or meat. Quite the opposite, many people are fascinated with snakes and want to keep them alive, even if it means removing them from the wild. In fact, the interest in snakes as exotic pets has grown so much that a great deal of money stands to be made by people who collect exotic snake species and sell them in their own countries or on the international market. Around the world, zoos and museums also collect snakes from the wild for display to the public.

Snakes are not always collected just for the benefits of humans. People remove some threatened species from the wild so that herpetologists can breed them in captivity. Many captive breeders hope that the snakes they breed will eventually be released to wild habitats, while some hope simply to preserve living specimens of snake species that may one day be extinct in the wild.

No matter what the reason for a snake's removal from the wild, the health of the remaining wild populations will be impacted. Because snakes' secretive nature makes them difficult to study in the wild, biologists cannot determine the exact impact that collection has on wild snake populations. They do know that collection reduces the number of mating pairs in the wild and that sustaining population numbers becomes more difficult for the snakes as a result.

The commercial pet trade

Herpetologist Chris Mattison says that for the pet trade alone, "tens if not hundreds of thousands of snakes change hands every year."[34] Though some commercial breeding operations have been set up in North America and Europe to supply the demand for snakes as pets, there is still a vigorous trade in wild snakes, resulting in problems for some species. According to Carl H. Ernst and George R. Zug, "Collecting for the pet trade has drastically reduced many populations."[35]

This often illegal collection of snakes from the wild is driven by several factors. For one thing, certain snake species are difficult to breed in captivity in numbers large enough to supply the demand for them. Also, the cost of captive breeding snakes often is significantly higher than the price a native collector charges for wild specimens. Moreover, snakes are relatively easy to ship, so long journeys from the wild to some collector's home does not contribute significantly to the cost of a wild specimen.

Most trade in snakes targeted for the pet market occurs in countries that have large numbers of species and where snakes are perceived as commonplace. For example, the snake trade is huge in Southeast Asia, especially Thailand, where people see snakes as a type of "crop" that can be harvested and sold for profit. Unfortunately, this belief in the plenty of wild snakes often leads their captors to have a complacent attitude about the animals and how they are housed and treated. As Mattison says, "Despite quite high prices of snakes at retail outlets, their value at source is small, leading to a complete lack of concern for their health and survival rate."[36] Oftentimes, large snakes are held in cramped, inadequate containers before they are shipped. Many experience stress or become so diseased that they die before reaching their destination.

As the most seriously threatened species become harder to find and more expensive to trade because of the legal restrictions on their capture and sale, many "common" species take their place on the exotic animal market. Incorrectly perceived as a limitless resource, the populations of these snakes also decline. A critic of the practice of trading in so-called common species, science writer Jean Lescure, says that many species of small boas and pythons are sold because the legislation controlling their capture and sale is less strict than that governing the sale of less common species such as cobras. Though its population numbers may have been stable, any species can quickly become threatened by overcollection.

Closer to home, overcollection has directly caused the decline of eleven of the fifty-six threatened and endangered snake species in the United States. The timber rattlesnake, for instance, has become a favorite of collectors, contributing to its decline, despite the fact that the U.S. government has added the rattler to the endangered list. Timber rattlesnakes are not alone. Herpetologist Harry W. Greene says that, despite federal laws against collecting threatened snakes, many people still "destroy many granite flakes [natural indentations in granite used by snakes as dens] and cap rocks in their search for California Mountain Kingsnakes (*Lampropeltis zonata*), Rosy Boas (*Charina trivirgata*), and other commercially valuable species."[37]

In some instances, commerce in endangered and threatened snakes still occurs in the United States because even

The Southern California coastal rosy boa pictured here is at risk because of overcollection of its species.

Collecting Snake Venom

To collect venom, a researcher positions a snake's fangs over the top of a vial and presses down on the venom sacs, milking the venom into the vial. After venom extraction, the snake's mouth is treated with an antibacterial spray and it is returned to its cage, where it will be fed a meal soon after.

Once collected, the venom is freeze-dried into a powder and is used either for medical research or to create antivenin, the antidote used to save the life of a snake bite victim. To create antivenin, the crystallized venom is injected in small amounts into another mammal, such as a horse. Over time, the horse's body will create antibodies to the venom. The horse's blood can then be drawn and the serum extracted, later to be injected into the body of a snake bite victim. The method is not entirely foolproof, however, because many people are highly allergic to horse serum.

A saw-scaled viper is milked for its venom, which will be used to create antivenin.

those officials responsible for protecting them mistakenly assume that most specimens came from captive-breeding populations. However, as Kenneth Dodd notes, "In most states, such as Florida with its wealth of unique species, commercial collection isn't regulated or monitored."[38]

Though much of the U.S. snake trade is regulated, there is still illegal trafficking in rare snakes such as the rock or Indian python and the gopher snake. According to Lescure, "This trade is not surprising, considering the great profits that can be gained from it. Some confiscated rock pythons must have brought their sellers $500 each on the North American market and would have been sold for up to $2,000 each to Japanese and European collectors."[39]

Snake experts like Larry Herrighty, the supervising wildlife biologist at the New Jersey Division of Fish, Game, and Wildlife, believe that the illegal snake trade goes on continually. Herrighty says, "We sometimes find people who are black-marketing these rare reptiles. It's a million-dollar business in the U.S."[40]

Working in cooperation with many state wildlife officials, the U.S. Fish and Wildlife Service has created programs to crack down on the illegal smuggling of endangered snakes. For example, a program called Operation Chameleon regularly catches and convicts people guilty of smuggling snakes into the country or illegally selling endangered and threatened native snake species. Speaking on behalf of such programs, Lois Schiffer, the assistant attorney general for environment and natural resources, says, "Trafficking in rare species threatens our environment. . . . Let the message be clear: We will take whatever steps are necessary here and abroad to stop the black market."[41]

Snakes that already face naturally occurring limitations are particularly vulnerable to exploitation by the exotic pet trade. For instance, on Queimada Granda, an island off the coast of Brazil, the endemic pit viper *Bothrops insularis*, has been listed as endangered as a result of overcollection. The species is vulnerable because females mate infrequently and have few offspring. By removing fertile adults from the wild, overcollection has turned this naturally low reproductive rate into a problem. Some scientists speculate that the snake's low reproduction might have doomed it to extinction regardless of human actions. But researchers M. R. Duarte, F. L. Franco, and G. Puorto conclude that, despite the fact that the snake has a low reproductive rate, "successive human actions over the decades, such as . . . the collection of hundreds of specimens in each expedition in a short time, may well have made this snake a threatened species."[42]

International regulations on trade

Many countries around the world have banded together to discourage the rising tide of illegal collection and export of endangered snakes. The same international organization that

The Illegal Snake Trade in the Soviet Republic

With the collapse of the Soviet Union has come laxity in the newly liberated republics toward trade in endangered animals, including snakes. In a July 1995 editorial in the *Herpetofauna News,* author Tom Langton notes, "Wildlife protection and management at the level of the [former soviet] republics are not clearly defined as yet, and existing programmes of wildlife conservation are not working." Laws designed to protect endangered snakes simply are not enforced. The thousands of endangered snakes not killed by inhumane collection and housing methods now move across the borders, finding their way to dealers in Europe and the United States. In the editorial, Langton notes, "It would be advantageous for the World Conservation Union to draw the attention of the republics to the alarming situation with the animal trade, and to request the governments of western countries to prohibit the import of Red Data Book species of amphibians and reptiles until these problems are resolved."

regulates trade in the skins of endangered snakes, CITES, also regulates trade in living specimens captured in the wild.

It is difficult to say how successful CITES has been in reducing trade in endangered snakes. For example, between 1972 and 1982, 228,416 legally collected live specimens of snake were exported to the United States. These figures, however, probably understate the problem that collecting presents for snakes since some threatened species are not listed under CITES. As herpetologist Kenneth Dodd says, "Although these species may have been exported legally, there are virtually no data on the status of any of them in the wild, so it is impossible to determine whether such trade has been detrimental to native populations."[43]

A problem directly related to this lack of data is that CITES regulations are too vague or difficult for trade officials in many countries to follow. For instance, one CITES regulation says that the shipper must certify that a snake is not threatened to such an extent in its country of origin that shipping it will endanger the health of the population. Since, in most cases, the data needed to verify a snake's status do not exist, shipping officials cannot make informed certifications. Moreover, officials often have no way of knowing whether a snake has been bred in captivity or collected from the wild, so illegally collected specimens can easily be misrepresented as captive bred.

Keeping snakes as pets is frowned on

Fueled in large part by this loosely regulated commercial trade, amateur snake-keeping is on the rise, further pressuring the populations of many species. Overcollection for sale to amateur keepers or collection by the amateur keepers themselves may well prove a species' downfall. For example, the eastern indigo snake, the largest and most harmless of North American snakes, declined in the wild as a direct result of overcollection by amateur enthusiasts. The eastern indigo snake once had large populations over much of the southern United States. Though it still has small populations in Alabama, Georgia, Florida, and South Carolina, the snake is now extinct in Mississippi because of overcollection. Its timidity and daytime hunting habits make it easy to catch, and its beautiful blue-black color makes it attractive to collectors. It also has a docile disposition and adapts well to captivity, making it all the more sought-after by those who like to keep snakes as pets.

The once populous eastern indigo snake has declined in great numbers due to overcollection and its popularity as a pet.

The small remaining wild population of the beautiful San Francisco garter snake has also been nearly eliminated by overzealous collectors who, until it was listed as a federally endangered species in 1973, caught as many of these rare specimens as they could find in the wild. Most of its habitat was completely destroyed to make way for airports and roads, and it is now restricted to the peninsula occupied by the city of San Francisco, California. Today, most of the remaining San Francisco garter snakes live in captivity.

Amateur Herpetologists as Captive Breeders

The number of endangered snake species considered as potential candidates for captive breeding is growing so rapidly that some proponents of the method believe it could be prudent to enlist the help of amateur herpetologists in the task. In his article "Future Role of the Private Sector in Breeding Endangered Species," anthologized in the book *Captive Management and Conservation of Amphibians and Reptiles*, snake expert Brian Brookner describes the type of people who might be involved: "The so-called private-sector is an extremely heterogeneous group. Education backgrounds can range from the professional with a postgraduate degree to the high school dropout."

To avoid the problem of amateurs collecting and keeping snakes illegally under the guise of captive breeding, many requirements would have to be put into place. Brookner says that all captive breeders would be required to attach passive integrated transponder (PIT) identification tags to cut down on the illegal trade of snakes. Brookner says that an endangered snake found without such identification would then be "presumed to be either illegally imported or collected, or to have had its PIT tag removed to obscure its origin."

Amateurs have not yet been encouraged to captive-breed endangered snakes. Brookner indicates that captive breeding by the private sector is still in the planning stages: "The future role of the private-sector in the breeding of rare and endangered species needs to be seriously considered, although implementation of a program . . . would be highly unorthodox by current practice and be likely to encounter stiff resistance by academics, zoo professionals, and law enforcement officers."

Many herpetologists openly criticize the practice of keeping and selling snakes as pets on the grounds that those who collect them do not properly care for them. As Ernst and Zug state, "Too often, snakes . . . are viewed as requiring minimum care rather than specialized care. The care provided is often inadequate and the reptile . . . soon dies or experiences ongoing suffering." Since the majority of snakes in the pet trade still come from wild populations, they suffer considerably in transit to the pet store. Ernst and Zug maintain that these snakes "are typically held and shipped in unsanitary and inhumane conditions. Many die, and most of the survivors arrive in ill health."[44] Even if snakes arrive safely at their destinations, if not properly cared for by their owners, they can develop maladaptation syndrome, a condition evidenced by a general decline in overall health. Maladaptation syndrome makes snakes abnormally vulnerable to bacteria, which can cause them to contract septicemia, pneumonia, and other similar diseases.

In an attempt to reduce the removal of endangered snakes from the wild, some U.S. states have passed tougher regulations. Under the Massachusetts Endangered Species Act, four snake species are listed as endangered: the worm snake, black rat snake, copperhead, and timber rattlesnake. The new regulations prohibit collecting or possessing any of these species without a special permit.

However, such legislation is not intended to completely discourage the practice of amateur herpetology. For instance, the Massachusetts legislation does allow people to capture up to two of each so-called common species of snake so that, according to herpetologists Scott Jackson and Peter Mirick, "budding biologists and snake enthusiasts could capture and study a few of the animals if they wished." Nonetheless, Jackson and Mirick, researchers at the University of Massachusetts, point out that many snakes do not adapt well to captivity. They maintain that

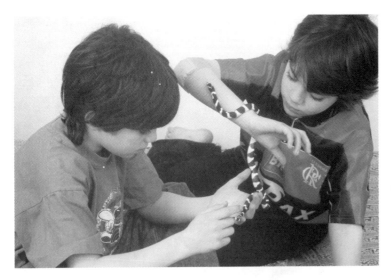

Eight-year-old twins play with their snake. Even though the practice of keeping snakes as pets is generally frowned upon, it is common.

"curiosity can generally be satisfied through a few days of observation, after which the snake should be released in the same place it was found."[45]

Those who catch and later release a snake must do so exactly where they found it because snakes are reliant on their knowledge of a small territory, and if released into unfamiliar territory, they may search aimlessly for prey or a den. As herpetologists Ernst and Zug note, "Moving a snake even a couple of kilometers might introduce it into a population with a differently adapted gene pool. If the released snake survives and reproduces, its genes might disrupt the local adaptation and decrease the probability of survival of subsequent generations."[46]

Even people who catch a snake from local populations near their home and plan to reintroduce it must be extremely careful how they handle the snake. There is a danger of transmission of parasites and viral or bacterial diseases if the snake is put in a cage that has contained diseased snakes. Once a diseased animal is released back into the wild, it can then transmit those diseases to others and severely impact a wild population.

Collecting snakes for captive breeding

Despite the belief that many snake species do not adapt well to captivity, some herpetologists believe that many endangered snakes risk extinction unless humans undertake an intensive program of captive breeding. Under such programs, individuals of a threatened or endangered species are removed from the wild and placed in protected environments that mimic their natural habitats. Although proponents of captive breeding believe that these snakes and their offspring can eventually be released back into the wild, in cases where no suitable wild habitat exists, snakes are simply kept in captivity to preserve a remnant of a species that would otherwise become extinct.

Many conservationists are leery of captive breeding, believing that such efforts may do more harm than good. They fear that collecting endangered species from the wild will further reduce the number of breeding pairs that will be adapted to living and reproducing in the wild.

Still others fear that captive-breeding programs direct attention away from the need for habitat protection. John Simmons, collection manager in the department of herpetology at the University of Kansas, pinpoints these concerns: "It's better to put resources of time and money into preserving habitat than in captive breeding. Without habitat preservation, the snakes have no future in the wild. We're left with very expensive, high-maintenance pets."[47]

Thomas Huff of the Reptile Breeding Foundation counters that, although habitat preservation is the preferred solution, it is not necessarily the practical one:

> Although we would prefer to see natural habitats preserved and the conservation of these rare animals in the wild, we accept the fact that many such efforts are futile, or, at best, delaying the inevitable extinction of these reptiles. . . . It is our hope that while we cannot prevent the extinction of these species in the wild, we may be able to prevent their total annihilation from the earth."[48]

 ## Genetic Consideration of Captive Breeding

Despite the risks that captive-bred specimens may pose to their wild brethren, these individuals offer some benefit to the species. Snakes born in captivity can contribute to the overall genetic health of an endangered species in the wild. The animals bred in captivity will ideally be used to revitalize the genetic makeup of the wild population through interbreeding.

The wild populations are equally important to the captive ones. Maintaining genetic diversity can make the difference between success and failure in a breeding program. Not all captive-breeding programs are successful at managing a genetically healthy population. In breeding the Madagascar ground boa in captivity, biologists have had less than 50 percent success in raising young snakes because of the limited genetic diversity among living specimens. In his article "The Husbandry and Propagation of the Madagascar Ground Boa *Acrantophis Dumerili* in Captivity" in the *ASRA Journal*, herpetologist Thomas Huff writes that "the number of independent blood lines is very low . . . indicating the possibility of captive stagnancy." This leaves little hope of releasing these individuals into the wild.

Huff feels that the captive breeding of endangered snakes such as the Madagascar ground boa must continue because preserving the snake's habitat in the hopes of reintroducing it to the wild does not seem feasible. He further argues that providing people with examples of living creatures now in man-made environments is more important than eventually displaying "just another example of an animal (represented by only a stuffed or pickled museum specimen) brought to extinction at the hands of man."[49]

Middle ground

Other herpetologists, such as Kenneth Dodd, take more of a middle position in the debate. Though Dodd does believe that too many captive-breeding programs are casually undertaken without thought for the future reintroduction of the species, he believes there is a solution to this problem. First and foremost, Dodd believes that a species should be captive bred only if it needs such propagation to prevent imminent extinction. Likewise, he feels that the ultimate goal of the program should be reintroduction to the wild. He suggests that program goals and a strict timetable for accomplishing them be written in the form of a species survival plan and that these goals be adhered to throughout the duration of the program. Additionally, the program's researchers should carefully record data and publish the results in reputable scientific journals.

Before individual snakes are removed from the wild, Dodd believes such programs should have proper facilities, adequate space, and the proper funding and staff needed to carry them through to reintroduction. Dodd further contends that people must be wholeheartedly behind such programs. If there is not enough support either financially or ideologically for a captive-breeding program, Dodd believes it should not be undertaken.

An essential aspect of any captive-breeding program is an examination and attempt to address the biological constraints that the endangered species will face in the wild after reintroduction. Potential release habitats must be studied to determine their freedom of movement; availability of basking sites, dens, and prey; and the presence of soils or

For some endangered snakes, like this Madagascar ground boa, captive-breeding programs may be the answer to increasing its numbers.

plants necessary to the snake's survival. Programs also need to assess the level of collection or commercial trade activity that could impact a snake reintroduced to a habitat.

The attempt to preserve the San Francisco garter snake provides an example of the sort of program Dodd envisions. Herpetologists John F. Cover Jr. and Donald M. Boyer believe that even though the San Francisco garter readily breeds in captivity, collecting snakes from the wild for captive breeding should be a last resort of preserving the species. Instead, they favor the creation of habitat reserves and rigorous enforcement of the federal government's Endangered Species Act. Though they approve of a captive-breeding program for the San Francisco garter snake, Cover and Boyer have very specific and limited goals for it. They do not believe that the program should be carried out solely for the purpose of reintroducing garter snake offspring to the wild. Instead, they want captive individuals to be used as public education ambassadors to raise public awareness of the snake's plight and of the need for preservation of its habitat.

The desire of many people to collect and breed snakes, though not an entirely proven or universal practice, does represent a shift in human attitudes toward snakes. This change in attitude has also been expressed in the form of habitat conservation, the adaptation of human activities harmful to snakes, education programs, and an increased interest in studying them.

5

Future Outlook

IN THE SECOND half of the twentieth century, some people began to reconsider their view of snakes. Many adopted the attitude expressed by herpetologist Harry W. Greene, that snakes are valuable even if they cannot provide a direct and easily observable benefit to humans: "Each of the more than 2,700 species of snakes embodies special relationships with its environment, and the earth would be poorer without them."[50]

One result of this new interest and appreciation of snakes is that people have sought to protect those that are particularly endangered by preserving their habitat. This is thought by conservationists to be the single most important step toward preventing mass extinction. More and more reserves, park areas, and conservation easements—privately owned property managed to preserve certain species and habitats—are being established specifically for snakes, which has not been the case in the past. This has meant that human developments that affect snakes have come under increasing public scrutiny.

Habitat preservation

For example, when a residential housing development in Evesham, New Jersey, threatened one of the few remaining habitats of the state's endangered eastern timber rattlesnake, the Pinelands Preservation Alliance (PPA), the New Jersey Audubon Society, and the Natural Resources Defense Council teamed up to file suit against the developer. Officials with the PPA learned that although the developer had indeed submitted the required herpetological survey of the planned development, he had neglected to report the obvious presence of the endangered timber rattlesnake on the property. A PPA report notes that several snakes had already been killed during construction of the first phase of the housing development. As a result of the negative publicity surrounding the proposed development in Evesham, the mayor and other city officials determined that open space preservation was of the utmost importance and committed themselves to working with environmental groups to ensure that the rattlesnake and its dwindling habitat receive protection.

A group called the Coalition to Save the San Francisco Garter Snake is waging a similar fight to protect the last remaining habitat of this severely endangered snake from further encroachment. The most recent battle involves the sale of the Cascade Ranch, near San Gregorio, California, to a developer who plans to build a campground and fitness resort over thirteen acres of one of the species' few remaining habitats. Construction of such a development would bring a glut of people and vehicles into the area. According to a press release by the San Gregorio Environmental Resource Center, which works in conjuction with the coalition, the U.S. Fish and Wildlife Service "acknowledges that several [San Francisco garter] snakes have been destroyed by vehicles in the area and so, for the present the coalition is requesting that no new roads be allowed to be built on Cascade Ranch and that vehicle traffic be restricted."[51] As George Cattermole, the director of the resource center, writes, "People must understand that at stake is the existence of a species. At stake is a chemistry and behavior which have survived for centuries, if not millennia in this beautiful area. . . . These species are barometers reflecting the health of our coastal environment."[52]

Habitat preserves have been set aside to protect two other federally protected species in the United States. Large portions of the delicate coastal habitat of Florida's endangered gulf salt

Various groups are working to protect the endangered San Francisco garter snake whose small numbers are a reflection of habitat loss.

marsh snake have been kept from development. The ridge-nosed rattlesnake also has received protection in New Mexico thanks to the Nature Conservancy, a conservation organization that seeks to preserve wildlife habitat in the United States and around the world by purchasing land that would otherwise be sold to developers. The conservancy purchased the Gray Ranch, a piece of property that includes a mountain range inhabited by the ridge-nosed rattlesnake. The organization then sold the property to a poet, Drum Hadley, who established the Animus Foundation, which agreed that the land would continue to be used for ranching while still maintaining the habitat to which the snake is adapted.

On the state level, plans have also been crafted to protect snakes like never before. For instance, Florida's Trust Preservation 2000 program provides grants to local communities to preserve fragile ecosystems and, as a consequence, some endangered species of snake such as the eastern indigo. Specifically, the King's Island Preserve in St. Lucie County contains 169 acres of mangrove swamps that have been preserved to improve the surface water quality and habitat for its creatures. One of the endangered species targeted for protection at King's Island is the Atlantic salt marsh snake.

In other countries around the world, people have begun to share this concern for snakes and their habitats. For example, China has set aside an entire island, called Snake Island, located south of Lüshun on the Liaodong Peninsula, to preserve the once threatened Pallas's pit viper. The island has been declared a nature preserve, and the snakes are fully protected. Thanks to this effort, the snake's population has risen to thirteen thousand individuals. Poland and the Czech Republic have cooperatively set aside a river valley preserve for the endangered tessellated snake that ranges across the borders of the two countries. Also, in Great Britain refuges for its threatened smooth snake have been established. In France, a small sanctuary has been set aside for the Orsini's viper in the Ventoux Mountains.

Legislation and agreements protect snakes

In some cases, enforcing legislation that protects individual snake species and their habitats is the only way that

Protection of Other Animals Protects Snakes

In some cases, an endangered snake's habitat is protected indirectly as a result of efforts to protect more popular birds or mammals that depend on the same habitat for survival. For example, the *Chironius vincenti*, or West Indian snake, needs the same large rain forest habitat as its more colorful and appreciated bird neighbor the St. Vincent parrot. In their July 1993 article "Status of the West Indian Snake *Chironius Vincenti*," herpetologists Robert W. Henderson and Gary T. Haas state, "Because of the protection afforded *A. guildingii* [St. Vincent parrot], and because of the national pride in the bird, *C. vincenti* will gain significant, direct benefits." A great deal of money has been spent on preserving habitat for the bird and conducting programs to educate local residents about it. Some of the preservation has, it seems, spilled over onto the West Indian snake as well since it was recently featured on a postage stamp.

Likewise, as people in the American Southwest try to preserve the dwindling habitat dens of the banner-tailed kangaroo rat, which have primarily been lost to development and ranching, the massasauga rattlesnake also benefits. The snake depends on the kangaroo rat's dens as a place to retreat from the intense heat of the sun and to regulate its body temperature.

conservationists can keep the snakes from becoming extinct and their habitats from being degraded. For example, the concho water snake, a species included on the threatened list in Texas, will remain on the list, according to the U.S. Fish and Wildlife Service, despite its establishment in new habitat areas. In the last half of the twentieth century, the snake's numbers declined initially because of a loss of its required stream habitat. More recently, construction of reservoirs in the area has flooded much of the snake's former range, and dams have prevented floodwaters from clearing settling silt out of the existing stream bed habitat. Buildup of silt allows vegetation to take root and choke out the shallow "riffle" habitat that young concho water snakes require.

Artificial riffle habitat designed by conservationists has provided some additional habitat for the remaining snakes but not enough, says the U.S. Fish and Wildlife Service, to warrant removing the species from the threatened list. When the U.S. Fish and Wildlife Service received a petition from the Colorado River Municipal Water District to remove the concho water snake from the threatened list in 1998, the service reevaluated the snake's former and current range. Nancy Kaufman, U.S. Fish and Wildlife Service regional director in Texas, says that, despite creation of new habitat areas, inadequate protection of stream flows in the Concho and Colorado Rivers still seriously endangers the snake and its fish prey. In the interest of protecting the snake, the U.S. Fish and Wildlife Service denied the water district's request that the snake be removed from the list.

In some cases, governments and industry representatives have worked together to create conservation agreements that will provide adequate protection for snakes before their habitats become so degraded that they have to be protected by endangered species legislation. This kind of solution benefits both snakes and people. For instance, a group of federal, state, and local legislators; coal-mining industry representatives; and farmers in Kentucky, Illinois, and Indiana formed a conservation team to protect the copper-belly water snake before its numbers fell to the point that it had to be listed as threatened. By their actions, this diverse group of people prevented a situation that would have resulted in the snake's remaining habitat being declared off-limits to virtually all human use.

The resulting conservation agreement involved the commitment of coal companies to stop or curtail mining in some key areas, modify some mining practices, and restore abandoned mining areas as habitat. Also, agricultural activities in some key habitat areas have been eliminated or modified to protect the snake. As Tom Bennett, commissioner of the Kentucky Department of Fish and Wildlife Resources, explains, "The agreement will ensure the continued existence of the species and the wetland ecosystems on which it depends. While the focus of this agreement is on the copper-belly water snake, many other bottomland, hardwood, and wetlands species will benefit. I hope this is the beginning of cooperative and proactive efforts to maintain healthy ecosystems for all species."[53] William R. Sprague, president of the Kentucky Farm Bureau, hails the agreement as "an important step toward taking away the adversarial stance between species protection and producers."[54]

The need for surveys and studies

Despite the difficulty of counting or studying them, the first step toward protecting snakes like the copperbelly is conducting surveys and studying each snake species carefully to determine the threats to it. One of the first challenges facing herpetologists is determining whether a species is endangered or threatened in the first place, and they must use a variety of tools to study the population health of these secretive animals. For the most part, herpetologists have had to rely solely on anecdotal accounts from local residents of sightings of particular snake species. These nonscientific data are hard to use as a measure of the health of a whole species, however. To overcome this difficulty, herpetologists try to measure these anecdotal reports against other information, such as a decline in previously heavy trade in a particular species of snake.

To determine the status of the timber rattlesnake in northern Wisconsin, state wildlife officials have used a combination of bounty records and anecdotal information from local residents to determine the snake's population status. The combined survey revealed that the snake's numbers

Bounty records and anecdotal information give researchers ideas of the number of timber rattlesnakes left in a given area.

were in steep decline. Herpetologists Gary Casper and Robert Hay say that both the bounty records and "interviews with retired snake hunters reveal that rattlesnake hunts decades ago routinely resulted in capture rates of 50 or 100 snakes per day. Today, biologists are rarely able to find more than 10 snakes per day."[55] Based on the results of this survey, scientists in Wisconsin and

Bounties' Days Are Numbered

The days of the government endorsing the slaughter of snakes may be numbered. Many U.S. states have reconsidered bounties and many have discontinued them. As people learn more about the value of snakes, even poisonous ones, to the larger ecosystem, bounties and roundups become a thing of the past. These shifts in attitudes have occurred in other countries as well. Herpetologist Chris Mattison notes in his book *The Encyclopedia of Snakes* that "a notable U-turn was taken by the Greek government who, in 1977, protected the endemic viper *Macrovipera schweizeri* (formerly regarded as *Viperalebetina schweizeri*) on Milos and a few neighbouring islands in the Cyclades group, having previously placed a bounty of 10 drachma on each snake."

neighboring Minnesota believe that if the snakes are not afforded protection, they could become seriously endangered.

Though herpetologists need more scientific evidence of a species' decline than anecdotal reports of sightings can provide, they say that such personal accounts can serve as a warning that something needs to be done. Anecdotal evidence of a species' decline may amount to nothing more than people reporting that they do not see as many of a particular species as they used to. For example, when questions about the distribution of the eastern indigo snake arose in Florida, researchers conducted interviews with people who were familiar with the snake in the area. This survey of residents helped biologists determine that the snake was distributed widely, though was not necessarily abundant throughout the area of Florida in question.

Kenneth Dodd says that once herpetologists have anecdotal evidence that a species might be endangered, they need to conduct extensive field research into its life span, habits, geographic distribution, and the threats facing it. Dodd warns against hasty, poorly researched claims that a species needs protection, saying, "An assessment of rarity is often a subjective judgment that reflects a lack of collecting effort or familiarity with appropriate habitats."[56] Furthermore, a species can be rare in one portion of its range but plentiful in another. Dodd says that protecting a supposedly rare species without scientifically assessing the health of its numbers may funnel already scarce conservation resources away from programs needed to protect snakes that are truly in trouble.

Because problems with these secretive creatures can occur gradually without human notice, many herpetologists suggest that all species, even those presumed "common," should be surveyed to determine overall numbers and head off any potential problems. With baseline numbers in place, herpetologists could then monitor a species' status and track the health of each individual population of that species over time. Herpetologist Howard K. Reinert describes the urgency of surveys of all species: "The fact is that, in many parts of the world, the snake fauna has not been fully investigated and we are undoubtedly exterminating some species before we even know of their existence."[57]

Once herpetologists decide which species are endangered or threatened, the next step they have to take is prioritizing which ones need immediate attention. Dodd says species should be prioritized from the rarest to the least rare. In general, the larger the distribution geographically, the less prone a species is to extinction. In other words, if more populations of a species are spread out over more land, it is less likely that the entire species will be wiped out by factors affecting just one isolated area of habitat. Also, knowing that certain species are naturally prone to decline because of factors such as short lifespans or low reproductive rates, herpetologists can focus their efforts and limited budgets on these species.

In Florida, a region that is rich in snake species but is becoming increasingly developed, snake species were prioritized based on surveys of their populations and habitat requirements. All snakes in the state were ranked by the Nongame Wildlife Program of the Florida Game and Fresh Water Fish Commission "so that priorities could be set about which species to protect first and what ecosystems in the area were most in need of protection."[58] By working this way, governments and researchers can put money where it is most urgently needed.

Habitat studies

An important area of research is how and why snakes select specific habitats. It takes many hours of research to understand a species' primary habitat as well as any seasonal habitats, where it moves in response to temperature changes, and the size and location of various populations. To date, habitat descriptions that are thorough and accurate have been created and recorded for only very few species.

As Reinert says, "The study of habitat use and selection by snakes is entering an exciting phase. The increased availability of unbiased sampling methods . . . is providing an unparalleled opportunity to examine the daily lives and behavioral patterns of these secretive animals under natural conditions."[59] With radiotelemetry, the process of transmitting information electronically, snakes can be tracked and monitored, providing researchers with a better idea of how and why they move about their habitat. There are two methods for attaching a radiotelemetry device to a snake. With smaller snakes, such as the San Francisco garter snake, researchers capture the snake and put a tiny plastic-coated radio chip into its mouth, which it then swallows. This lodges in the intestine, allowing researchers to determine the snake's location and body temperature until the snake consumes a meal and the chip is passed out with body waste. To track larger snakes, such as the bushmaster, researchers must capture the snake and surgically implant the chip inside its body cavity.

For those snakes with special habitat requirements, including foraging areas, dens, or other retreats from sun or cold, researchers will

Researchers implant a radiotelemetry device in a rattlesnake. Such devices allow researchers to learn extensively about a snake's habitat.

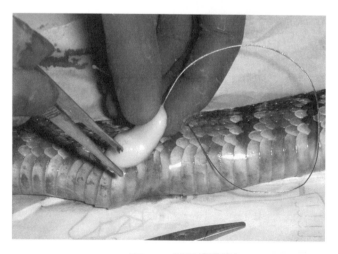

need to provide careful, ongoing monitoring and management of their habitats. For instance, timber rattlesnakes that hibernate in dens have been carefully observed. One study revealed that to ensure continued healthy reproduction in this threatened species, logging practices in the study area would have to be altered. Though male timber rattlesnakes had little difficulty existing in heavily logged areas, gravid—that is, pregnant—females required much denser stands of trees, which were scarce in the study area.

Due to extensive research on the Florida pine snake's habitat, the future looks brighter for the conservation of this species.

Similarly, researchers made interesting discoveries when studying the habitat of the Florida pine snake. Whereas male pine snakes cannot have overlapping territories, females can. When land for snake habitat is set aside, these requirements must be considered. Study results also indicated that in order for population numbers to grow, the conservation program must accommodate a much larger number of Florida pine snakes. This, in turn, will require larger areas of undisturbed habitat than originally thought.

Some promising habitat preservation programs developed in response to such surveys are on the horizon. A trend toward comprehensive land-use plans have been considered in communities with heavy snake populations so that development can proceed with snake species in mind. Dodd says that in Florida,

> for example, each . . . county is required by state law to develop a comprehensive land-use plan through the year 2000. Examination of these plans reveals that little habitat will remain undeveloped in some counties if the plans are implemented. Knowledge of such microdistribution is essential to ensuring that planners are aware of unique species and communities before conflicts arise.[60]

"Generally overlooked"

The biggest deterrent to future snake studies and habitat conservation remains the fact that most people do not like snakes. Generally, snakes make headlines only when a person is bitten. On the other hand, as Dodd says, "when it comes to bad things happening to snakes, however, few supportive resources are available. . . . When conservation funds are handed out, amphibians and reptiles are generally overlooked, and funds for snake conservation are extremely rare."[61]

Though the general public is generally in favor of protecting more popular species, such as wolves and bald eagles, they are rarely moved by the plight of snakes. To cite just one example of this attitude, herpetologist Harry W. Greene says that "visitors surveyed at a national park in the eastern United States overwhelmingly supported protection of 'all wildlife' but were much less enthusiastic about a later question as to whether snakes in the park should be killed."[62]

Educating the fearful

In general, the more people learn about a wild creature, the less they fear it. This is the reality fueling many snake education projects around the world. Amateur herpetological societies, zoos, and snake parks all have been founded in an effort to educate the public, especially children, about these fascinating creatures. For instance, the British Herpetological Society formed the Young Herpetologists Club and hired an education officer to encourage children to take an interest in snakes in general and to become involved in practical conservation projects.

Governments too have stepped in to educate the public about endangered snakes living near their homes. In Aruba, the endangered Aruba Island rattlesnake is still living in the wild, and there is potential for release of more individuals raised under a captive-breeding program. However, the government knew that if the people were not educated about the snakes, they might kill them or destroy critical habitat. Likewise, an education program sponsored by the American Association of Zoological Parks and Aquariums toured U.S. schools to teach children about their local rattlesnakes. To reach adults, the association conducted a public relations campaign that included informational stories in newspapers and magazines and on television and radio. As a result of the program, many people began to see rattlesnakes in a new

Some Conservationists Dislike Snakes

Even some conservationists have problems tolerating snakes and do not understand or appreciate their role in the larger ecosystem. If it is hard to convince a bird-watcher to like a snake, it is even more difficult to convince the average person who does not appreciate nature to such an extent. The following quote from Harry W. Greene's book *Snakes: The Evolution of Mystery in Nature* describes just such a snake-skeptical bird-watcher.

> For more than forty years Alexander F. Skutch has studied the bird life of tropical forests in Costa Rica, and he is especially well known for his careful, descriptive accounts of nesting biology. . . . Skutch grudgingly allows for predators in distant wilderness areas, but prefers a "principle of harmonious association" for his own surroundings, one in which "every member is compatible with every other, and there is mutual exchange of benefits." To that end he kills Bird Snakes (*Pseustes Poecilonotus*), Tiger Ratsnakes (*Spilotes pullatus*), and other harmless species and singles them out to explicate a strange worldview. After dismissing danger to humans as a justification for killing these predators, Skutch wrongly claims that snakes are never "really social" and notes that with few exceptions, they are "devoid of parental solicitude."

light, believing they had a right to coexist with people. Similarly, to protect the highly endangered Virgin Islands boa, the U.S. Fish and Wildlife Service has attempted to educate the public about the species on the islands of Puerto Rico and St. Thomas. It has tried to show area residents that the boa will not harm them and will actually benefit them by controlling rodent populations.

With time and education, people have learned to tolerate and even appreciate snakes. Rattlesnake expert Curt Brennan is evidence of such a change. Though he once took the prize for killing the greatest number of timber rattlesnakes in a Pennsylvania roundup, he is now one of their greatest allies. As he began to study the snakes, he began to change his perspective about how they should be treated. He now believes that the snakes are "shy, retiring and exceptionally fragile, easily injured by the rough handling they receive in capture . . . and disappearing from many of the haunts where they'd once been common."[63]

Many conservationists believe that adults and children alike must be educated about snakes and their declining habitats in order to create empathy for the animals.

Brennan still hunts for timber rattlesnakes but only for purposes of observation.

In an interview with author Scott Weidensaul, Brennan explains how he came to view timber rattlesnakes as creatures needing protection from the unnecessary and cruel practice of rattlesnake roundups:

> I can't stand being a fake, and I was helping to perpetuate a lie by portraying myself as a rough, tough saver of mankind by rounding up rattlesnakes. And I knew that the snake population was in trouble if I, and others like me, continued to do what we were doing. Just by getting close to the animal, and being around it for a very short time, you learn that they're not what people have led you to believe they are. If you give yourself two minutes to calm down, you'll learn that the animal isn't out to get you—it's out to get away from you.[64]

Herpetologist Greene hopes that people will eventually follow suit with this former rattlesnake hunter and feel about snakes as they do many other species now protected and appreciated in a variety of habitats around the world. He says, "With increased understanding, we too might even afford them a place in modern landscapes. I look forward to a day when park rangers will proudly guide visitors to a Timber Rattlesnake den, when nature tourists will travel to Arizona or Costa Rica with hopes of seeing several species of pitvipers on one trip."[65] Unfortunately, if current trends continue, a significant number of snake species may be lost before this attitude takes hold.

Notes

Introduction

1. Carl H. Ernst and George R. Zug, *Snakes in Question: The Smithsonian Answer Book.* Washington, DC: Smithsonian Institution, 1996, p. 142.

Chapter 1: What Is a Snake?

2. Eric S. Grace, *Snakes.* San Francisco: Sierra Club Books for Children, 1984, p. 50.

3. Quoted in Ernst and Zug, *Snakes in Question*, p. 57.

4. Ernst and Zug, *Snakes in Question,* pp. 33–34.

Chapter 2: Dwindling Snake Habitat

5. Robert H. Mount, *The Reptiles and Amphibians of Alabama.* Auburn, AL: Auburn University Agricultural Experiment Station, 1975, p. iii.

6. Quoted in Richard A. Siegel, Joseph T. Collins, and Susan S. Novak, eds., *Snakes: Ecology and Evolutionary Biology.* New York: Macmillan, 1987, p. 493.

7. Quoted in Richard A. Siegel and Joseph T. Collins, eds., *Snakes: Ecology and Behavior.* New York: McGraw-Hill, 1993, p. 379.

8. Jonathan K. Webb and Richard Shine, "Out on a Limb: Conservation Implications of Tree-Hollow Use by a Threatened Snake Species (*Hoplocephalus bungaroides:* Serpentes, Elapidae)," *Biological Conservation*, July-August 1997, p. 31.

9. Richard Shine et al., "The Impact of Bush-Rock Removal on an Endangered Snake Species, *Hoplocephalus Bungaroides* (Serpentes: Elapidae)," *Wildlife Research*, no. 25, 1998, p. 294.

10. Paul E. Moler, ed., *Rare and Endangered Biota of Florida*, Vol. 3. Gainesville: University Press of Florida, 1992, p. 161.

11. Harry W. Greene, *Snakes: The Evolution of Mystery in Nature*. Berkeley and Los Angeles: University of California Press, 1997, p. 299.

12. Quoted in Craig Pittman, "Fire Ants Ravaging Threatened Species," *St. Petersburg Times*, November 15, 1999. www.sptimes.com/News/111599/news_pf/State/Fire_ants_ravaging_th.shtml.

13. Mount, *The Reptiles and Amphibians of Alabama*, p. iii.

14. Greene, *Snakes*, p. 300.

Chapter 3: Direct Killing of Snakes

15. Quoted in Scott Weidensaul, "The Belled Viper," *Smithsonian*, December 1997, p. 100.

16. Chris Mattison, *The Encyclopedia of Snakes*. New York: Facts On File, 1987, p. 172.

17. Quoted in Roland Bauchot, ed., *Snakes: A Natural History*. New York: Sterling, 1997, p. 212.

18. Quoted in Bauchot, *Snakes*, p. 211.

19. Quoted in Bauchot, *Snakes*, p. 211.

20. Quoted in Siegel, Collins, and Novak, *Snakes*, p. 499.

21. Denise Sewell, "Illegal Entry," *E/The Environment Magazine*, May-June 1997. www43.rapidsite.net/emagaz/may-june_1997/0597curr_1.html.

22. Quoted in Bauchot, *Snakes*, p. 211.

23. Ernst and Zug, *Snakes in Question*, p. 143.

24. Greene, *Snakes*, p. 77.

25. Weidensaul, "The Belled Viper," p. 108.

26. Weidensaul, "The Belled Viper," p. 108.

27. Romulus Whitaker, "Population Status of the Indian Python (*Python Molurus*) on the Indian Subcontinent," *Herpetological Natural History*, July 1993, p. 87.

28. Whitaker, "Population Status of the Indian Python (*Python Molurus*) on the Indian Subcontinent," p. 89.

29. Greene, *Snakes*, p. 285.

30. Humane Society of the United States, "The Harmful Effects of Rattlesnake Roundups." www.hsus.org/programs/wildlife/hunting/rattlesnakes.

31. Weidensaul, "The Belled Viper," p. 106.

32. Anne Cordeiro, "Snake Charms Liberty County Man," *Savannah Morning News*, December 28, 1999. www.savannah morningnews.com/ns-search/smn/stories/122899/LOC snakes.shtml.

33. Quoted in Weidensaul, "The Belled Viper," p. 99.

Chapter 4: The Complications of Collection

34. Mattison, *Encyclopedia of Snakes*, p. 172.

35. Ernst and Zug, *Snakes in Question*, p. 150.

36. Mattison, *Encyclopedia of Snakes*, p. 115.

37. Greene, *Snakes*, p. 299.

38. Quoted in Siegel, Collins, and Novak, *Snakes*, p. 497.

39. Quoted in Bauchot, *Snakes*, p. 211.

40. Quoted in Timothy May, "Owner of Exotic Snakes Probed," *NRAAC News*, July 3, 1998, p. 1.

41. Quoted in U.S. Department of Justice, Office of Public Affairs, press release, "Reptile Smuggler Sentenced for Trafficking in Rare Species," April 16, 1999. www.usdoj.gov/opa/pr/1999/april/140enr.htm.

42. M. R. Duarte, G. Puorto, and F. L. Franco, "A Biological Survey of the Pitviper *Bothrops Insularis* Amaral (Serpentes, Viperidae): An Endemic and Threatened Offshore Island Snake of Southern Brazil," *Studies on Neotropical Fauna and Environment*, March 1995, p. 1.

43. Quoted in Siegel, Collins, and Novak, *Snakes*, p. 498.

44. Ernst and Zug, *Snakes in Question*, p. 150.

45. Scott Jackson and Peter Mirick, "Protection of Snakes." www.umass.edu/umext/snake/prot.html.

46. Ernst and Zug, *Snakes in Question*, p. 151.

47. John Simmons, interview by author, November 11, 1999.

48. Thomas Huff, "The Husbandry and Propagation of the Madagascar Ground Boa *Acrantophis Dumerili* in Captivity," *ASRA Journal*, 1983, p. 50.

49. Huff, "The Husbandry and Propagation of the Madagascar Ground Boa *Acrantophis Dumerili* in Captivity," p. 52.

Chapter 5: Future Outlook

50. Greene, *Snakes*, p. 305.

51. San Gregorio Environmental Resource Center, press release. http://members.aol.com/Wharfmag/snake.htm.

52. Quoted in San Gregorio Environmental Resource Center, press release.

53. Quoted in U.S. Fish and Wildlife Service, press release, "State, Federal, and Private Groups Sign Agreements to Protect the Copperbelly Water Snake," January 27, 1999. http://darwin.eeb.uconn.edu/Documents/fws-970127.html.

54. Quoted in U.S. Fish and Wildlife Service, press release.

55. Gary Casper and Robert Hay, "Timber Rattlesnake Status." www.mpm.edu/collect/vertzo/herp/timber/status.htm.

56. Quoted in Siegel and Collins, *Snakes*, p. 365.

57. Quoted in Siegel and Collins, *Snakes*, p. 122.

58. Quoted in Siegel and Collins, *Snakes*, p. 367.

59. Quoted in Siegel and Collins, *Snakes*, p. 233.

60. Quoted in Siegel and Collins, *Snakes*, p. 367.

61. Quoted in Siegel and Collins, *Snakes*, p. 363.

62. Greene, *Snakes*, p. 292.

63. Quoted in Weidensaul, "The Belled Viper," p. 99.

64. Quoted in Weidensaul, "The Belled Viper," p. 100.

65. Greene, *Snakes*, p. 287.

Glossary

antivenin: The antidote created from snake venom to treat snake-bite victims.

arboreal: A word used to describe a tree-dwelling snake.

aposematision: The distinctive bright colors or patterns that advertise to potential predators that an animal is poisonous or distasteful to eat.

basking: The process by which a snake raises its body temperature by finding a sunny spot to absorb heat.

bounties: Monetary rewards given to hunters in exchange for physical proof of having killed a "nuisance" animal.

captive breeding: The process by which both amateur and professional herpetologists raise and breed snakes in captivity either to sell or to release back into the wild.

CITES: Convention on International Trade in Endangered Species of Wild Flora and Fauna; countries all around the world use this regulation to monitor trade in live animals and animal products.

cloacal vent: The opening through which a snake's wastes are emitted and where reproduction occurs.

dermis: The inner layer of skin just beneath a snake's scales.

dry bite: A bite in which a snake does not inject venom.

ectotherm: An ectotherm is an animal whose body temperature reflects the external temperature in its environment.

endemic: A word used to describe an animal known to live only in one particular area.

epidermis: The outer layer of a snake's skin that, at its outer edge, produces scales.

exotic species: An animal not known to have lived in an area until humans introduced it there.

gravid: A pregnant snake.

habitat corridors: Narrow passages of preserved habitat meant for snakes to use for getting from one habitat patch to another.

herpetology: The study of reptiles.

Jacobson's organ: The organ inside a snake's mouth that its tongue rubs over to transfer chemical signals to the brain, which are communicated as scents.

keels: Ridges along a snake's scales that assist it in moving along the ground.

keratin: The protein that makes up a snake's scales and the hooves, nails, and hair of other animals.

microhabitat: A small, confined habitat that changes little in temperature from season to season.

neurotoxin: A venom that attacks its victim's central nervous system.

oviparous: A snake that lays eggs.

radiotelemetry: The process by which scientists attach tags to snakes and then track them from remote locations by radio.

rattlesnake roundup: Organized hunts, primarily in North America, in which people try to force rattlesnakes from den sites and then kill or relocate them.

spectacle: The scale covering a snake's eye.

thermoregulation: The process by which a snake or other reptile moves to different locations in its environment to either raise or lower its body temperature.

viviparous: A snake that gives birth to live offspring.

Organizations
to Contact

Chicago Herpetological Society
Membership Secretary
2060 N. Clark St.
Chicago, IL 60614
(773) 281-1800
http://207.105.50.158/.

A group of herpetologists and reptile enthusiasts, the goals of this organization are to educate the public, promote conservation, and advance herpetology. Members have the opportunity to learn about herpetology and participate in studies.

Gainesville Herpetological Society
PO Box 140353
Gainesville, FL 32614-0353
http://gnv.ifas.ufl.edu.

The Gainesville Herpetological Society acts as a forum of communication for anyone interested in herpetology. It promotes the scientific study and conservation of amphibians and reptiles worldwide and welcomes new members.

Herpetologists League
College of Arts and Sciences
Florida International University
North Miami, FL 33181
www.inhs.vivc.edu.

Established in 1936, the Herpetologists League is an international organization of people devoted to studying the biology of amphibians and reptiles.

Kansas Herpetological Society
18683 W. 160th Street
Olathe, KS 66062
(913) 397-8143
eagle.cc.ukans.edu/~cnaar/chsmain.html.

The society is a nonprofit organization established in 1974 and designed to encourage education and the spread of herpetological information; the conservation of wildlife, specifically of amphibians and reptiles; and to promote information sharing between herpetologists.

Society for the Study of Amphibians and Reptiles
PO Box 626
Hays, KS 67601
(314) 977-3658
www.ukans.edu/~ssar.

Founded in 1958, this not-for-profit group advances research, education, and conservation of reptiles and amphibians. The largest international herpetological society, it is recognized around the world for having the most diverse program of publications, meetings, and other activities.

Suggestions for Further Reading

Books

Caroline Arnold, *Snake*. New York: Morrow, 1991. Arnold has a reputation for writing excellent, easy-to-understand books about animals, and this one is no exception. She takes great care to include photographs illustrating the points she makes in the text as well.

Eric S. Grace, *Snakes*. San Francisco: Sierra Club Books for Children, 1984. This book provides beautiful illustrations of species and interesting information not found in volumes simply discussing snakes in general.

Grolier World Encyclopedia of Endangered Species. 10 vols. Danbury, CT: Grolier, 1993. This reference set is an excellent place to find photographs and detailed information about endangered snakes around the world.

J. M. Roever, *Snake Secrets*. New York: Walker, 1979. Though a bit outdated, this is a good first reference book for students who want to learn about the natural history, habits, and habitat of snakes.

Internet Sources

American Society of Ichthyologists and Herpetologists www.utexas.edu.depts/asih.

American Zoo and Aquarium Association http://aza.org.

Colorado Herpetological Society http://coloherp.org.

Massachusetts Division of Fisheries and Wildlife
www.umass.edu.

Texas Parks and Wildlife
www.tpwd.state.tx.us/nature/endang/.

U.S. Fish and Wildlife Service
www.fws.gov/r3pao/eco_serv/endangrd/news.

Works Consulted

Books

Roland Bauchot, ed., *Snakes: A Natural History*. New York: Sterling, 1997. An excellent all-around text for the person who wants to learn about not only the natural history of snakes but also their influence on man throughout history.

J. C. Daniel and J. S. Serrao, eds., *Conservation in Developing Countries: Problems and Prospects*. Bombay, India: Oxford University Press, 1990. Though limited in the information it includes about snakes, this is still a useful discussion of the problems facing animals in developing countries.

Carl H. Ernst and George R. Zug, *Snakes in Question: The Smithsonian Answer Book*. Washington, DC: Smithsonian Institution, 1996. This is a wonderful volume. It is divided into sections headed by common questions asked by people about snakes.

Harry W. Greene, *Snakes: The Evolution of Mystery in Nature*. Berkeley and Los Angeles: University of California Press, 1997. A nice blend of scholarly discussion and personal anecdotes about the author's experience with snakes during his work as an anthropologist.

Les Line, ed., *What We Save Now*. Boston: Houghton Mifflin, 1973. Though this anthology was published in the 1970s, the experiences of its contributors as they travel in the wild places of the United States is still interesting reading.

Chris Mattison, *The Encyclopedia of Snakes*. New York: Facts On File, 1987. More than most other books on the subject, this one carefully describes the natural history of many of the world's species of snakes.

Paul E. Moler, ed., *Rare and Endangered Biota of Florida.* Vol. 3. Gainesville: University Press of Florida, 1992. Though obviously narrow in its focus on Florida snake species alone, it still gives excellent information on species that live in Florida but that also have populations outside the state.

Robert H. Mount, *The Reptiles and Amphibians of Alabama.* Auburn, AL: Auburn University Agricultural Experiment Station, 1975. Admittedly, this book is dated, but the information about habitat destruction and the need for conservation areas is just as valid today as when it was written.

James B. Murphy, Kraig Adler, and Joseph T. Collins, eds., *Captive Management and Conservation of Amphibians and Reptiles.* Ithaca, NY: Society for the Study of Amphibians and Reptiles, 1994. This book does a good job of discussing the various views about captive reproduction and covers many programs already in progress.

Richard A. Siegel and Joseph T. Collins, eds., *Snakes: Ecology and Behavior.* New York: McGraw-Hill, 1993. This sequel to *Snakes: Ecology and Evolutionary Biology*, offers more up-to-date information on the status of many species.

Richard A. Siegel, Joseph T. Collins, and Susan S. Novak, eds., *Snakes: Ecology and Evolutionary Biology.* New York: Macmillan, 1987. This anthology features excellent articles on conservation and surveys and is written primarily by university professors of herpetology.

K. F. Stoker, *Medical Use of Snake Venom Proteins.* Boca Raton, FL: CRC, 1990. Not recommended for the average reader, this extremely difficult and scholarly book does offer interesting information about experimental uses of snake venom in human medicine.

Alan Ternes, ed., *Ants, Indians, and Little Dinosaurs.* New York: Charles Scribner & Sons, 1975. Though outdated, this book celebrates the 75th anniversary of *Natural History* magazine and includes some of the best scientific articles published in the journal between 1900 and 1975.

Periodicals

G. Scott Allen and Karel Fortyn, "The Central Asian Cobra, *Naja oxiana* (Eichwald, 1831): Maintenance in Captivity and a Report of a First Captive Breeding," *Bulletin of the Chicago Herpetological Society*, July 1992.

Warren Bates, "Cedar Glen Man Stands Up and Fights for Tiny Snake," *San Bernardino Sun*, July 28, 1984.

Mark Bavetz, "Geographic Variation, Status, and Distribution of Kirtland's Snake (*Clonophis Kirtlandii* Kennicott) in Illinois," *Transactions of the Illinois State Academy of Science*, vol. 87, No. 3–4, 1994.

Q. M. C. Bloxam and S. J. Tonge, "The Round Island Boa *Casarea Dussumieri* Breeding Programme at the Jersey Wildlife Preservation Trust," *Dodo*, Nov. 23, 1986.

Massimo Capula, Lorenzo Rugiero, and Luca Luiselli, "Ecological Observations on the Sardinian Grass Snake, *Natrix Natrix Cetti*," *Amphibia-Reptilia*, May 1994.

John F. Cover Jr. and Donald M. Boyer, "Captive Reproduction of the San Francisco Garter Snake *Thamnophis Sirtalis Tetrataenia*," *Herpetological Review*, vol. 19, no. 2, 1988.

George H. Dalrymple and Norman G. Reichenbach, "Management of an Endangered Species of Snake in Ohio, USA," *Biological Conservation*, no. 30, 1984.

Michael Dekker, "KDOT: Harm from U.S. 59 'minimal,'" *Lawrence Journal World*, November 19, 1999.

M. R. Duarte, G. Puorto, and F. L. Franco, "A Biological Survey of the Pitviper *Bothrops Insularis* Amaral (Serpentes, Viperidae): An Endemic and Threatened Offshore Island Snake of Southern Brazil," *Studies on Neotropical Fauna and Environment*, March 1995.

Economist, "From Cattle Prods to Cobras," January 25, 1997.

Johannes Foufopoulos and Anthony R. Ives, "Reptile Extinctions on Land-Bridge Islands: Life-History Attributes and Vulnerability to Extinction," *American Naturalist*, January 1999.

Robert W. Henderson and Gary T. Haas, "Status of the West Indian Snake *Chironius Vincenti*," *Oryx*, July 1993.

Thomas Huff, "The Husbandry and Propagation of the Madagascar Ground Boa *Acrantophis Dumerili* in Captivity," *ASRA Journal*, 1983.

Christopher Joyce, "Busted: America's Snake Smugglers," *New Scientist*, August 1981.

Michael J. Lacki, Joseph W. Hummer, and Joyce L. Fitzgerald, "Application of Line Transects for Estimating Population Density of the Endangered Copperbelly Water Snake in Southern Indiana," *Journal of Herpetology*, June, 1994.

Tom Langton, "Commercial Collecting as a Threat for Amphibian and Reptile Species of the Former Soviet Union," *Herpetofauna News*, July 1995.

————, "Conservation status of a rare viper on Queimada Grand Island, Brazil," *Herpetofauna News*, July 1995.

Sergei Mamet and Sergei Kudryavtsev, "Breeding Latifi's Viper (*Vipera Latifii*) at Moscow Zoo," *Snake*, September 1996.

Timothy May, "Owner of Exotic Snakes Probed," *NRAAC News*, July 3, 1998.

Donald McNeil Jr., "One African Takes Fangs over Fido as a Sentry," *New York Times*, February 9, 1997.

Paul E. Moler, "Distribution of the Eastern Indigo Snake, *Drymarchon Corail Couperi*, in Florida," *Herpetological Review*, vol. 16, no. 2, 1985.

J. C. Murphy, "Atlantic Salt Marsh Snake Listed as Threatened," *Chicago Herpetological Society Newsletter*, February 1978.

Paul F. O'Connor, "Captive Propagation and Post-Copulatory Plugs of the Eastern Indigo Snake," *Vivarium*, October, 1991.

Jayanta Sarkar, "Handle with Care: India's 'Snake Man' Warms Up to His Cold-Blooded Charges," *Far Eastern Economic Review*, April 3, 1997.

Stacey Schultz, "Snake Oil Success," *U.S. News & World Report*, June 1, 1998.

Carolyn Shea, "Ask Audubon: Is It True That the Taipan Is the World's Deadliest Snake?" *Audubon*, September/October 1999.

Richard Shine et al., "The Impact of Bush-Rock Removal on an Endangered Snake Species, *Hoplocephalus Bungaroides* (Serpentes: Elapidae)," *Wildlife Research*, no. 25, 1998.

Richard Shine and Mark Fitzgerald, "Conservation and Reproduction of an Endangered Species: the Broad-Headed Snake, *Hoplocephalus Bungaroides* (Elapidae)," *Australian Zoologist*, September 1989.

Peter J. Tolson, "Captive Breeding and Reintroduction: Recovery Efforts for the Virgin Islands Boa," *Endangered Species Update*, November 1990.

Jonathan K. Webb and Richard Shine, "Out on a Limb: Conservation Implications of Tree-Hollow Use by a Threatened Snake Species (*Hoplocephalus bungaroides*: Serpentes, Elapidae)," *Biological Conservation*, July-August 1997.

Scott Weidensaul, "The Belled Viper," *Smithsonian*, December 1997.

Romulus Whitaker, "Population Status of the Indian Python (*Python Molurus*) on the Indian Subcontinent," *Herpetological Natural History*, July 1993.

Internet Sources

Africa Reptile Page, "Rainbow Boas." www.webtronics.co.za/rainbow.htm.

Gary Casper and Robert Hay, "Timber Rattlesnake Status." www.mpm.edu/collect/vertzo/herp/timber/status.htm.

Anne Cordeiro, "Snake Charms Liberty County Man," *Savannah Morning News*, December 28, 1999. www.savannahmorningnews.com/ns-search/smn/stories/ 122899/LOCsnakes.shtml.

Humane Society of the United States, "The Harmful Effects of Rattlesnake Roundups." www.hsus.org/programs/wildlife/ hunting/rattlesnakes.

Scott Jackson and Peter Mirick, "Protection of Snakes." www.umass.edu/umext/snake/prot.html.

Kevel Lindsay, "Caribbean Racers: Antiguan Racer May Be on the Rebound." www.frontiernet.net/˜rsajdak/antigua.htm.

Pinelands Preservation Alliance, "Pinelands Preservation Alliance Hot Issues: The Sanctuary and Timber Rattlesnakes." www.pinelandalliance.org/issues/rattlesnakes.html.

Craig Pittman, "Fire Ants Ravaging Threatened Species," *St. Petersburg Times*, November 15, 1999. www.sptimes.com/News/ 111599/news_pf/State/Fire_ants_ravaging_th.shtml.

Todd Randall and Stuart Poss, "Species Summary for *Nerodia clarkii clarkii*." www.ims.usm.edu/˜musweb/ nerodcla.htm.

Darlene Rigg, "Snakes of Indiana." http://birch/palni.edu/˜ drigg/snakes.htm.

San Gregorio Environmental Resource Center, press release. http://members.aol.com/Wharfmag/snake.htm.

Denise Sewell, "Illegal Entry," *E / The Environment Magazine,* May-June 1997. www43.rapidsite.net/emagaz/may-june_1997/ 0597curr_1.html.

Texas Parks and Wildlife, "Endangered and Threatened Species." www.tpwd.state.tx.us/nature/endang/animals/ conchows.htm.

Eileen Underwood, "Tidbits of Information: Dumeril's Boa," *Cold Blooded News*, April 1999. http://coloherp.org/ cb-news/cbn-9904/DumerilsBoa.html.

U.S. Department of Justice, Office of Public Affairs, press release, "Reptile Smuggler Sentenced for Trafficking in Rare

Species," April 16, 1999. www.usdoj.gov/opa/pr/1999/april/140enr.htm.

U.S. Fish and Wildlife Service, press release, "State, Federal, and Private Groups Sign Agreements to Protect the Copperbelly Water Snake," January 27, 1999. http://darwin.eeb.uconn.edu/Documents/fws-970127.html.

Wildlife Information and Rescue Service, "Broad-Headed Snake, *Hoplocephalus Bungaroides*." www.streetnet.com.au/wires/3210.htm.

Index

Picture Credits

About the Author

Kelly L. Barth is a freelance writer who lives in Lawrence, Kansas, near the tallgrass prairie, one of the world's endangered habitats. In addition to writing, she volunteers at a wildlife rehabilitation clinic, where she works with snakes.